RHYTHMS OF REVIVAL

The Spiritual Awakening of 1857–63

Ian M. Randall

D1492928

Paternoster:
thinking faith

16 15 14 13 12 11 10   7 6 5 4 3 2 1

First published 2010 by Paternoster
Paternoster is an imprint of Authentic Media Limited
Milton Keynes
www.authenticmedia.co.uk

British Library Cataloguing in Publication Data

A catalogue record for this book is available from the
British Library

ISBN 978-1-84227-721-8

Design by Philip Miles
Printed and bound in Great Britain by Bell and Bain, Glasgow

Contents

Foreword   v

Acknowledgements   ix

1. Spiritual Revival and Quickening   1

2. The Power of Prayer   9

3. The Role of Ministers   29

4. Emerging Evangelists   49

5. Youth Taking Part   70

6. Church Renewal   88

7. The Gospel in Society   108

8. Conclusion   125

Endnotes   129

Select Bibliography   148

Foreword

As a ten year old I remember attending a meeting where Duncan Campbell was the speaker and he spoke about the unique events that had occurred in the parish of Barvas on the Island of Lewis – what came to be termed the Hebrides Revival (1949–52). I can recall the unusual stillness of the congregation as he spoke and the quiet enthusiasm of my parents after the meeting. I knew the message had touched their hearts in some significant way. The only illustration I recall from Duncan Campbell's message is the story of the pub that closed when revival came to a town. Later, as a young pastor, I read that one of Campbell's repeated emphases was captured in the saying: 'Revival is a community saturated with God. Revival is God moving into the district.'

I was also privileged in my teenage years to hear first-hand accounts of the mid-twentieth-century East African Revival from speakers such as Joe Church and William Nagenda. As a family we attended the annual conferences organized by Roy Hession and Stanley Voke, and my early discipleship years were imbued with some of the principles of spiritual revival. I record my gratitude to God for this spiritual cradle of nurture in discipleship.

As I reflect on almost fifty years in Christian ministry, I can observe how revival teaching has been one of the shaping influences of my discipleship and Christian leadership. Subsequently other streams of renewal have flowed into my life, many of them focused on the renewal of the Church as a mission-intentional faith community and the prophetic role of the Church in the public square. For this reason I appreciate the way Ian Randall poses the question in this book of how the Church can bring together a commitment to spiritual renewal and social change.

The great value of *Rhythms of Revival* is the reminder that 'there are times in the story of the Church that are notable' and the book draws us to consider the abiding lessons of one significant period of revival. There is a refreshing lack of emphasis on formulae and a sound critique of any undue concentration on the phenomena of revival. Ian Randall's distinct focus is the consideration of the major dynamics of a single-period revival movement. The author draws on his rich resource of historical knowledge and offers some unique insights into revival rhythms – the place of prayer, the role of pastors, the empowering of lay people, the revitalizing of worship and the impact on young people and children.

Kingsley Apiaghei, the pastor of the very large Trinity Baptist Church, London, and currently the President of the Baptist Union of Great Britain, has an infectious passion for calling churches to expect revival and he exhibits in his fruitful life and ministry that revival is not a hopeless dream but a living reality for God's people *today*. I know that Ian Randall shares the conviction that spiritual revival is for *today*, and his own warm-hearted spirituality means that he has not simply written this book from the grandstand as an historical observer. Ian wants to stimulate the reader to observe the unique context in which we find ourselves in the second decade of the twenty-first century. As he says, 'Revival always occurs within particular contexts, and the rhythms of revival . . . are worked out in unique ways.'

The Church in the UK has experienced decades of laudable initiatives in church renewal, which have undoubtedly strengthened the spiritual life of churches in key areas, such as worship, discipleship, fellowship, mission and evangelism. Millions of pounds have been expended on transforming old church buildings into fit-for-purpose mission centres for the twenty-first-century Church. We have proved to ourselves that we can organize great events; we can mobilize effective community projects and harness the spiritual enthusiasm of thousands of young people who volunteer for ministries in all parts of the globe.

But in this same period of spiritual renewal there has been a steady fall in church attendance and a steep moral decline in the culture; we face an erosion of Christian influence in society so that, as one commentator has suggested, there is now 'a cold climate' for the Church in its public witness. Charles Haddon Spurgeon (frequently cited in this book) in one of his memorable sermons on revival called for a spiritual life that would *purify the age.* He longed for a Church that would have more power and influence for righteousness, social reform and moral progress. This is the revival message that resonates with me and I hope this book will set your mind and heart flowing in the same direction.

David Coffey
President of the Baptist World Alliance
Advent 2009

Acknowledgements

I wish to express my gratitude to all those who have helped me in my thinking about rhythms of revival. I am thankful, too, that through many friends and through several Baptist and other Christian communities of which I have been a part I have experienced significant times of spiritual renewal. I am indebted to a number of ministers and teachers for their inspiration and guidance in this area from my period of formative Christian experience in the 1960s onwards: William Still, Martyn Lloyd-Jones, Erroll Hulse, Barrie White, Douglas McBain and David Coffey in particular.

Coming closer to home, I want to say thank you to my family for all their love and support – to Ailsa and Jiří, to Moragh and Skander, and above all to my wife Janice, who, as always, has read carefully through and commented on my draft material. Others have also helped in this way – especially Sharon James, who read an early version.

I have been able to discuss some of this material with colleagues in different settings and I have greatly benefited, once more, from being involved in stimulating theological communities in London and Prague – Spurgeon's College and the International Baptist Theological Seminary (IBTS). I presented one chapter of the book at an IBTS Research Seminar. My thanks, also, to David Emmanuel Singh in Oxford for carrying an article on this topic in *Transformation* (Vol. 26, No. 4, 2009), the journal he edits.

It was through an approach from Steve Brady, Principal of Moorlands College, that I wrote this study, and I am thankful to Steve, whose experiences have coincided with my own at many points, for his encouragement. My attempt to write about rhythms of revival is part of my commitment to engaging with the history of movements of evangelical spirituality, and in seeking to do this I owe much to the academic example and the friendship of David Bebbington, Professor of History at Stirling University. Finally, I wish to thank Robin Parry and other colleagues involved in the publishing process for their expertise.

This book is dedicated to my grandchildren, Theodore and Iona.

Ian M. Randall
Cambridge
Advent 2009

1

Spiritual Revival and Quickening

I was introduced to the subject of revival in the late 1960s, initially through coming to know about, and then soon after that
through hearing, the preaching of Dr Martyn Lloyd-Jones,
who was for almost thirty years the very influential minister of
Westminster Chapel, London.[1] In the 1970s I was a member of
Cuckfield Baptist Church, in Sussex, and the minister, Erroll
Hulse, to whom I owe a great deal, was someone who was
greatly concerned for authentic spiritual revival. Erroll Hulse,
who was himself indebted to Lloyd-Jones, has written help-
fully on the subject of revival – on biblical, historical and contemporary issues – in his book *Give Him No Rest* (from the text,
'You who call upon the LORD, give yourselves no rest, and give
him no rest till he establishes Jerusalem and makes her the
praise of the earth, Isaiah 62:6b, 7). This is a book that, like
many other books written, and also sermons delivered, by
evangelicals, is designed to encourage prayer for revival.[2]

Two of the general books on revival that I have found most
useful overall, for their combination of historical material and
theological reflection, are: Brian Edwards, *Revival!: A People
Saturated with God* (1990), and R.E. Davies, *I Will Pour Out My
Spirit* (1992).[3] Also invaluable are the studies undertaken by
Edwin Orr, who did more detailed historical work on the history of revival worldwide than any other person during the
course of the twentieth century. I have found his accounts,
which include *The Second Evangelical Awakening in Britain*
(1949) and *The Fervent Prayer* (1974), most informative and
have made extensive use of them.[4] As David Bebbington
points out, Orr does not tend to distinguish between local,

spontaneous awakenings and carefully organized evangelistic meetings.[5] On the other hand, he makes very fruitful connections between different movements. I am indebted to the work of two students at Spurgeon's College, Roger Welch and Ian Hare, who wrote dissertations on aspects of revival in the nineteenth century.

What is revival? R.E. Davies defines it in this way:

> A revival is a sovereign outpouring of the Holy Spirit upon a group of Christians resulting in their spiritual revival and quickening, and issuing in the awakening of spiritual concern in outsiders or formal church members; an immediate, or, at other times, a more long term, effect will be efforts to extend the influence of the Kingdom of God both intensively in the society in which the Church is placed, and extensively in the spread of the gospel to more remote parts of the world.[6]

It is this approach to revival that I will be following. I will not be attempting to give systematic attention to the socio-economic factors that may or may not have contributed to the shaping of revival movements. These are not unimportant, but I follow Richard Carwardine's caution about attempts to explain revival 'as a product of a particular set of political or socio-economic conditions'. Carwardine argues that the only stable factor among the whole complex set of influences on revival has been 'a climate of opinion that regarded revivals as desirable'.[7] At the same time, I recognize – as Philip Sheldrake has put it – that 'spirituality is never in pure form'. There is always a context that shapes what takes place.[8] In looking at revival, I am not focusing on mission enterprises, except inasmuch as they flow out from revival movements. Nor am I looking at organized 'revivals'. In 1901, a leading North American evangelist, R.A. Torrey, wrote a book, *How to Promote and Conduct a Successful Revival*. That kind of evangelistic event, or 'revival', is not my topic.[9]

I see the history of the Church through the centuries as following the pattern suggested in an analysis by Martyn Lloyd-Jones when he preached a series of sermons on the subject in 1959. These sermons were stimulated by a desire to call

to mind the Revival that had happened a hundred years before
– a revival period that will be the focus of this book. Lloyd-
Jones argued that the history of the Church has not been a
straight line, but that there have been significant ups and
downs. Times of revival and reawakening were followed by
periods when the Church was lacking in life.[10] The idea of
cycles or waves of revival did not start with Lloyd-Jones. In the
eighteenth century, Jonathan Edwards promoted this idea.[11] In
Wales, William Williams, Pantycelyn, was also speaking in the
same period about cycles of renewal and decline.[12] This understanding is examined in Richard Lovelace's outstanding book,
Dynamics of Spiritual Life;[13] and in an excellent study of the
Revival of 1857–58 in North America, Kathryn Long has
shown that by the mid-nineteenth century the 'cyclical' view
of revival, which was especially the product of the Calvinist
theological tradition, had been adopted and developed by a
number of influential writers. This approach 'maintained the
supernatural character of revivals and affirmed the role of
Providence in superintending the future of the church and the
[North American] nation, yet at the same time allowed considerable leeway for human activity.'[14] The longer history of the
Christian Church is also a story that includes periods of revival
and resurgence.[15]

Although writers in the past have never, as far as I know,
used the term 'rhythms of revival', it seems to me that this is
what the advocates of the cyclical model were indicating: that
there is a spiritual ebb and flow. Lloyd-Jones spoke – and also
warned – about what happened when there was less evidence
of the life of the Holy Spirit in the Church. Church services, in
such times, he suggested, were often marked by 'a smug con-
tentment'. Then, in times of revival, there was a return to the
vivacity seen in the New Testament.[16] I have found a suggestion made by Brian Edwards very illuminating: that all the
elements of revival are normally present in the life of the
Church. The members of any local church are (for example)
engaged in praying, seeking holiness, worshipping and wit-
nessing. But in revival these elements are heightened and
intensified. What is new is the way in which Christians in the
churches pray, worship and witness. There is fresh life and

power. However, the major features that characterize the life of the Church remain largely constant. There are 'old things with new life'.[17]

A number of books on revival try to construct a theology of revival from the Bible. Clearly there is much in the Bible about authentic spiritual life. The situation of Israel in the Old Testament, however, is not the same as that of the Christian Church in the era of the Holy Spirit, and the New Testament introduces us only to the early years of the Church. There is a fascinating anticipation in Acts 3:20: 'that times of refreshing may come from the presence of the Lord', which may suggest future seasonal blessing of a special kind.[18] But the biblical material does not deal to any great extent with the condition of churches that have, over a period of time, lost their spiritual authenticity and whose need is to be revived. Perhaps something of that is found in the warnings to the churches in the book of Revelation.

Those who have looked at revival theologically have a valuable contribution to make. Stuart Piggin, who is a fine historian, attempted to do this in his *Firestorm of the Lord*.[19] Criticisms have been made of this approach.[20] I have found Iain Murray's suggestion in *Pentecost – Today?* helpful: that the 'outpourings of the Spirit' in the book of Acts, rather than being uniformly present in the subsequent history of the Church, belong to recurring 'creative epochs'. Murray quotes from George Smeaton, a nineteenth-century Free Church of Scotland minister (a professor in Aberdeen and then in Edinburgh), who observed that when 'a former awakening has spent its force' then 'a new impulse is commonly communicated' by God.[21]

Justified criticisms of some approaches to revival have been made. In the book, *On Revival: A Critical Examination*, contributors offer thoughtful essays that are worth serious attention. Nigel Wright, for example, seeks to highlight the difference 'between an act of God that comes freely and sovereignly, sometimes with strange wonders attached, and the human propensity to help it on its way by the use of suggestion and the power of psychic energy'.[22] There are also attempts to secure revival through human acts of obedience, a position criticized by Murray.[23] In similarly critical – and, in my view, very helpful

– vein, Ian Stackhouse, in his book *The Gospel-Driven Church* (2004), has written of the deleterious features of a revivalist mentality within a section of contemporary evangelicalism, and in an essay in the volume *On Revival*, he argues: 'Susceptibility to only the latest and the sensational demonstrates an adolescent spirituality; one that is demonstrably ill prepared for the vagaries and mundanities of normal Christian living.' He suggests that a fascination with novelty weakens the 'tenacity and perseverance' that are needed within charismatic-evangelical communities today in rising to the missional challenge.[24]

I like the realism of the words 'vagaries and mundanities'. In Christian experience, it is important to accept the place of the ordinary as well as the extraordinary. Alongside this, I find the idea of 'seasons' in the Christian journey a valuable one. The language of 'seasons' implies a degree of predictability, and at the same time variety, but not usually novelty. I am using 'rhythms' in a way that is close to the idea of 'seasons'. Similarly, John Colwell, in his creative study, *The Rhythm of Doctrine*, looks at theology through the lens of the worship of the Church, which follows the seasons of the Christian year.[25] Again, Nigel Wright, reflecting on periods of 'intense spiritual experiences', suggests that such experiences 'can give way, perhaps must give way, to a barrenness of spirit. After mountain-top experiences, where is there to go but back into the valley? And perhaps this must be so, since God is always greater than the experiences we have of him and therefore our experiences need to drop away so that we are dealing with God himself'.[26] The concept of a rhythm in wider spiritual experience – of communities as well as individuals – coheres with this perspective.

In this book I will be probing some of the dynamics of revival, while never suggesting that there is any formula that can produce a movement of the Spirit. God's work is not subject to human control. In utilizing the idea of rhythms, I am thinking of the way the rhythms in music are expressed in different notes. I will attempt to explore some of the 'notes' by looking at the movement of revival and its aftermath in evangelical churches in the period from the later 1850s to the early

1860s. There have been varied assessments of the effects of the revival movement of this period. John Kent argues that in the period 1857 to 1862 there was 'a last major outburst of popular feeling' of a pietist nature in North America and the north of Ireland, but he contends that 'in England attempts to encourage similar signs of revival failed almost completely' and that the so-called 'Revival' was only significant in that for the last time as a national phenomenon, the 'traditionally Puritan areas [North America and the north of Ireland] went through the phases of being convicted of sin, brought to repentance and finally converted'.[27] Others have disputed this interpretation. Janice Holmes has argued, on the basis of detailed research, for the ongoing existence of revival in the sense of 'a spontaneous outpouring of the Holy Spirit'.[28] John Coffey has shown the significant impact of nineteenth-century revival movements.[29]

David Bebbington has argued that over time various models of revival have been evident within Protestantism – Presbyterian, Congregational, Methodist, synthetic, modern and global. In the twentieth century, Bebbington notes, 'the epicentre for much of the global spread was the Welsh Revival of 1904–05'.[30] I am particularly interested, at a time when there is awareness of the benefits and challenges of being a global village, in how the Christian community worldwide has developed a sense of its worldwide identity. A great deal of fine work has been done on the 1904–5 experience, including its international dimensions,[31] and interest was especially generated when the centenary of the Welsh Revival was being celebrated. I am interested in how some of the developments of this early twentieth-century period contributed to the rise of Pentecostalism, which since then has been the most rapidly growing part of the wider evangelical world.[32] In 1960, a new period in the history of the Church began, with the worldwide charismatic movement.[33] But the movement of revival that began in 1857, which was an evangelical movement that had a global reach and which contributed elements to be found in the later movements, has not, in recent years, been given as much attention as I believe it deserves.

I suggest that the transatlantic and to some extent global Revival of the period 1857 to 1863 offers important insights into the nature of evangelical renewal, drawn as they are from a period when the evangelical movement was playing a crucial role in the worldwide Christian community – as it does today, particularly because of the growth of Pentecostalism. The development of evangelical Christianity from the eighteenth century to the 1990s is being traced in six outstanding volumes being published by Inter-Varsity Press. The volume covering the period examined here is by David Bebbington, who shows that the years from the 1850s to the 1900s can properly be viewed as years when evangelicalism, with its emphases on the Bible, the cross, conversion and activism, had a dominant place in Protestant Christianity.[34] This is not to suggest that evangelicalism in this period was uniform. There were theological divisions between Anglicans and Nonconformists, Baptists and Paedobaptists, Calvinists and Arminians. But there was a shared identity. I will be looking at evangelicals as a whole, rather than seeking to separate out various subgroups. My own view is that the evangelical movement is at heart a spiritual tradition, and that from the perspective of spirituality there has been much that evangelicals have held in common.[35]

One of the many examples of different evangelicals joining together in the period of revival being studied here comes from Wales. In Festiniog, an Anglican clergyman, R. Killin, wrote in 1860 about how news came in early 1859 of revival in North America, South Wales and Ireland. As a result, weekly prayer meetings were arranged. Killin wrote:

> Between the 7th of September and the 10th of October [1859], when the revival broke out like a torrent which carries everything before it, the deepest feeling was manifested in my congregations . . . A large open-air prayer-meeting was held in one of the quarries, which deeply affected many. Some young people broke out rejoicing, in a prayer-meeting held amongst themselves in one of the chapels. There was an unusual solemnity of feeling in church, and some of my people assembled in a cottage afterwards, and held a prayer- meeting, which continued until midnight. The week following, prayer-meetings were held in every place of worship every night of the week.

Killin spoke of many people joining churches belonging to different denominations.[36]

The year 1859 was widely celebrated, in 2009, as the year in which Darwin wrote his famous *On the Origin of Species*. This was also the year when Karl Marx published a trial volume of what was afterwards rewritten as *Das Kapital*. Significant changes in thinking were taking place in this period, as is also the case today, with world views in a state of flux in many societies. But rather than concentrating simply on 1859, I look at a longer period of renewal, lasting for about six years, with 1859–60 as the mid-point. There was an increasing spiritual intensity among many evangelicals up to that mid-point, but the effects were also powerful in the years that followed. I am seeking to offer an analysis of what I see as major dynamics in the period – with chapters looking at prayer, the role of ministers, the contribution of lay people, the place of young people and children, the effects on church life and the wider impact. All of these shaped, and have continued to shape, the rhythms of revival.

2

The Power of Prayer

The mid-nineteenth-century Revival, which occurred in North America, in the period 1857 to 1859 especially, and contributed to significant spiritual advance in North America and elsewhere, has often been known as 'the prayer meeting Revival'. This was a revival that affected churches in several countries, but the emphasis on prayer meetings – often large-scale meetings – has been associated especially with events in North America. It seems that in the mid-1850s in the USA the spiritual life in many of the churches was far from vibrant and that there had been decline for several years. Kathryn Long, noting that this Revival has received far less attention than earlier revivals, sees it as 'perhaps the closest thing to a truly national revival in North American history'.[1]

The impact of revival in this period was far from being confined, however, to North America. There were powerful movements in Ireland, Scotland, Wales and England. At the heart of this spiritual renewal was a belief in prayer and a conviction that revival would spread through prayerful waiting in God's presence. Thus evangelicals in the north of Ireland joined those in London in praying for that city, and in consequence Samuel Garratt, a leading Anglican evangelical in London, expected (as recorded in one of the books about the Revival in Britain, *Authentic Records of Revival, Now in Progress in the United Kingdom*) a 'great outpouring of the Spirit' among London's population.[2] Prayer was central.

The prayer meeting Revival

One of the most widely read books about the North American Revival was *The Power of Prayer* (published 1858) by Samuel Irenaeus Prime, a Presbyterian minister who became editor of the *New York Observer*.[3] In his telling of the story, Samuel Prime focused on Jeremiah Lanphier (born in 1809 and converted to Christ at the Broadway Tabernacle in 1842). Lanphier was a businessman who in 1857 had become a city missioner with the North Church (Dutch Reformed) in New York. As he prayed about his ministry, Lanphier became more and more encouraged in 'the joyful expectation God would show him the way, through which hundreds and thousands might be influenced on the subject of religion'.[4] Lanphier's work was directed more to visiting 'the sick and the poor' than to businessmen, but he had the idea of providing a noonday prayer period for the business community. He mentioned the idea, but received little support.[5] This is what he wrote:

> Going my rounds in the performance of my duty one day, as I was walking along the streets, the idea was suggested to my mind that an hour of prayer, from twelve to one, would be beneficial to *business-men*, who usually, in great numbers, take that hour for rest and refreshment. The idea was to have singing, prayer, exhortation, relation of religious experience, as the case might be; that none should be required to stay the whole hour; that all should come and go as their engagements should allow or require, or their inclinations dictate. Arrangements were made, and at twelve o'clock noon, on the 23rd day of September, 1857, the door of the third storey lecture-room was thrown open. At half-past twelve the step of a solitary individual was heard upon the stairs. Shortly after another, and another; then another, and, last of all, another, until six made up the whole company! We had a good meeting. *The Lord was with us to bless us.*[6]

The midday prayer meetings started in Fulton Street, New York, in an upstairs room of the Dutch Reformed Church Consistory Building. Lanphier printed handbills and invited businessmen, mechanics, clerks – different classes of people –

to join in prayer.[7] Soon the numbers coming for prayer increased. William C. Conant, in a book written in 1858, *Narratives of Remarkable Conversions*, described how daily prayer meetings began (on 23 September 1857), how 'the meeting-room overflowed and filled a second, and eventually a third room in the same building; making three crowded prayer-meetings, one above another, in animated progress at one and the same hour'. Other venues were taken. The John Street Methodist Church and lecture-room were both opened for daily noon prayer meetings, by a committee of the Young Men's Christian Association, and were soon crowded. Meetings moved outside the churches, to Burton's Theatre in Chambers Street.[8]

Events in the wider society had a significant impact. A financial crisis in North America followed a boom year in which speculators made large amounts of money. On 24 August 1857, the respected Ohio Life Insurance and Trust Company collapsed. A month later depositors stormed banks in Philadelphia, and in New York the stock market crashed. There was widespread panic. Tens of thousands of people lost their jobs. It is significant, against this background, that the group most associated with the prayer meetings was of businessmen. The *Journal of Commerce*, a financial paper, suggested in November 1857 that readers might 'steal away from Wall Street and every worldly care, and spend an hour about mid-day in humble, hopeful prayer'.[9] On 5 January 1858, Lanphier visited the offices of daily newspapers to seek to interest them in the prayer meetings, and a month later widespread press coverage began in the *New York Herald* and *New York Tribune*. Massive growth in the meetings took place: the newspapers were soon reporting that over six thousand were attending the daily prayer meetings in New York. To some extent the press contributed to the growth. Prayer meetings in Philadelphia started as small gatherings but on 6 March 1858 the Philadelphia press gave the meetings front-page coverage and over the course of a week the numbers in Jayne's Hall increased from three hundred to at least four thousand.[10] In many places those who were not yet committed Christians began to attend the prayer meetings. The rhythm of revival then moved from prayer to outreach.

News about this prayer movement across the Atlantic quickly reached Ireland, which had many links with North America through the large numbers of Irish people who had emigrated there. There was a fresh stirring of prayer in the north of Ireland in the period when the prayer meetings began in New York, and also, at the same time, a growth of evangelical activity, especially among Presbyterians.[11] On hearing about the Revival in New York, the Irish Presbyterians sent two senior ministers to find out more. One of the two, William Gibson, later wrote about his experience and about what happened in Ireland in his book, *The Year of Grace*.[12] Gibson, as a Professor of Christian Ethics and Moderator of the General Assembly of the Presbyterian Church in Ireland, was someone whose opinion carried considerable weight. He wrote that for many months after his return he spoke to congregations across the north of Ireland about 'what he had seen and heard of the great work of God during his transatlantic visit'. His statements, he reported, were received 'with the deepest interest' and he felt that the attention he received was a 'harbinger' of something 'no less glorious' than he had seen in North America.[13] Here the transmission of concern for revival across national boundaries is evident.

The beginnings of the Revival in the north of Ireland have, as Janice Holmes notes, been associated with four young Irishmen, who began to hold a weekly prayer meeting in a school in the village of Kells, not far from Ballymena, County Antrim. The four were James McQuilkin, John Wallace, Robert Carlisle and Jeremiah Meneely. Holmes speaks about the 'semi-mythologised' beginnings, especially in relation to the role of McQuilkin, who was a handloom linen weaver.[14]   Samuel J. Moore, Presbyterian minister in Connor and Kells, in an account published in Belfast in 1859, identified these four, with their 'Believers' Fellowship Meeting' – which began in September 1857 – as crucial to the spiritual movement that took place. Moore's account was used by John Weir (Presbyterian minister in Islington, London) in his book *The Ulster Awakening*, published in 1860. Moore's and Weir's narratives placed emphasis on 'the power of prayer' beginning to be 'known, and felt, and seen', with several dramatic conversions taking place.[15]

Gibson, in his book, published a year earlier, had noted the 'four young men whose names have been much before the public in connexion with the subsequent revival', but insisted that 'the first stirrings of life' came earlier, from a Presbyterian Sunday school prayer meeting,[16] while William Arthur, a leading British Methodist, who was originally from Kells, described how the 'small farmers, weavers and linen manufacturers' of the parish of Connor were deeply affected and added that 'everywhere faith in prayer, mighty prayer, seemed the first and deepest lesson of the Revival'.[17] The movement in these rural communities was in marked contrast to the urban beginnings in North America.

In Scotland the Revival seems to have begun in the autumn of 1858, again through prayer meetings. A period of concerted prayer began in Aberdeen on 1 September 1858, with one of the factors being the news of the North American revival. Developments are outlined by Kenneth Jeffrey in his comprehensive analysis of the 1858–62 Revival in the north-east of Scotland. He writes that a group of young men began to meet for prayer in Aberdeen and within about a week united prayer meetings were being held daily in the city's County Buildings, with six hundred attending. An itinerant evangelist, Reginald Radcliffe (who was a lawyer), was invited by William Martin, the Professor of Moral Philosophy at Marischal College, Aberdeen, to conduct evangelistic meetings. These led to conversions. The minister of Greyfriars Church, Aberdeen, reported that 'the blessing descended in large measure'.[18] By the middle of the following year large prayer meetings were being held in Glasgow. J. Barbour Johnstone, the revered Free Church of Scotland minister in Wolflee, in the Scottish border country, writing of a visit to the Wynd Church (later St George's Tron Church) in Glasgow, said: 'There is a meeting held there also every evening. I had seen many deeply affected and weeping bitterly there. But the last evening evidently a great work was wrought. There was great solemnity during the prayer meeting – many deeply impressed.'[19] Horatius Bonar, the hymn writer and one of the best-known Free Church ministers of the period, commended these and other reports that were brought together in *Authentic Records of*

Revival. Bonar wrote that 'the authenticity and genuineness of the matter it contains are removed entirely from the region of dubiety by getting ministers to give narratives of the work of the Spirit of God as they themselves have seen it in its manifestations and results among their people'.[20]

It appears that there was a heightened desire for prayer in parts of Wales in the summer of 1859. Developments were traced by Thomas Phillips in *The Welsh Revival: Its Origin and Development* (1860). One of those seeking a movement of renewal was Thomas Aubrey, a Wesleyan Methodist minister who had been influenced by the North American preacher, Charles Finney. But Aubrey became ill before the Revival reached its full force.[21] More central was Humphrey Jones, who had emigrated from Wales to the United States and had become a missionary with the Methodist Episcopal Church. Having been involved in the Revival there in 1857, he returned to Wales anxious to see a movement of the Holy Spirit in his homeland. Humphrey Jones stressed the importance of an awakened Church and the necessity of earnest prayer. Another leader was David Morgan, a Calvinistic Methodist preacher who was transformed by the Revival. When David Morgan first heard Jones preach and talked to him, he was uncertain – even sceptical – but what Jones said to him had such a powerful effect that he could not sleep for several nights, and he prayed for guidance about what to do. Eventually Morgan concluded, without much enthusiasm: 'We cannot do much harm by keeping prayer-meetings, and trying to rouse the country.' Jones, replying, expressed his conviction that 'if you try it will not be long before God will be with you'. This proved to be the case.[22]

The beginning of the prayer revival in England can probably be traced to united prayer meetings in London, initially in the Cosby Hall, in August 1859. Soon attendance at this meeting reached one hundred and similar meetings began in the much larger Exeter Hall, an evangelical centre in London. By the end of the year twenty-four prayer meetings were being held daily and sixty were being held weekly in the London area. The Earl of Shaftesbury (Lord Shaftesbury), the outstanding evangelical social reformer of the period, was committed to this prayer movement. Services were held in churches and other large buildings across the country, such as in the Grand Theatre, Croydon, and special prayer meetings began in many parts of England – in villages in the counties of Devon and Cornwall (with their strong revival tradition), in Kent, in the Midlands and in the north-west. C.H. Spurgeon, who had emerged as the most popular British Baptist minister of the time, had at this point been preaching for five years in London to very large crowds, but for him the new impetus in 1859 was significant. In December 1859, he wrote:

> The times of refreshing from the presence of the Lord have at last dawned upon our land. Everywhere there are signs of aroused activity and increased earnestness. A spirit of Prayer is visiting our churches . . . The first breath of the rushing mighty wind is already discerned, while on rising evangelists the tongues of fire have evidently descended.[23]

This is how the rhythms of revival are often described.

Orderly prayer

In seeking to understand the place of prayer in revival it is not enough simply to say that prayer is important in spiritual awakening. That is certainly true. A study of the rhythms that have characterized past revivals suggests, however, that there have been different types of prayer in different movements in history. This awareness of variety can help to avoid the idea that there is a prayer 'formula' that can produce revival. Whereas it is sometimes thought that prayer linked with revival has always been both emotional and extended, the Revival in North America and in a number of other places was marked, in most cases, by orderly prayer meetings. It is true that in Wales, and to a lesser extent in parts of Scotland, the prayer meetings were less structured than in North America. It is also true that in some meetings – especially in the north of Ireland – there were physical 'manifestations', such as people falling down and crying out for forgiveness. The more dramatic physical expressions in Ireland, however, were not typical of the Revival meetings as a whole. I will look at the significance of these phenomena, and the views of church leaders about them, in the next chapter. Here I want to focus on the organization of the prayer meetings in North America, while recognizing that what happened in the European context was not a replica of the North American experience.

A 'plan of meeting' that was adopted at the meetings in the North Dutch Church in Fulton Street, New York, had considerable influence on the shaping of revival prayer meetings not only in the city of New York, but also in many other places. It seems that the intention in the Fulton Street meetings was to achieve a balance that allowed freedom but guarded against disorder and disharmony. Samuel Prime reproduced the wording of a typical notice used at the John Street Prayer Meetings in New York. This says:

> 1st.—HYMN, not over four stanzas.   2nd.—READING SCRIP-
> TURES, never over fifteen to twenty verses.   3rd.—PRAYER by
> Leader.

> These three exercises, not to occupy over twelve minutes; then
> the meeting to be left open for prayer or exhortation. No person
> to pray or exhort over three minutes, nor pray and exhort the
> same day. At half-past twelve o'clock the leader will ask any
> who wish the prayers of the meeting for themselves to rise
> without speaking, and remain standing a few seconds—a half
> minute being allowed for this. At the touch of the bell will begin
> a season of two minutes' silent prayer, to be broken by the
> leader asking some brother by name to lead in prayer. It is
> desired that no more than two consecutive prayers or exhorta-
> tions should follow each other. When a verse of any hymn is
> desired to be sung, let it be announced distinctly, that all may
> find it, as it may not be familiar—to each one, and never over
> two verses at a time. When special requests for prayer are read
> by the leader or made by the audience, let them not be disre-
> garded by the one who next leads in prayer. The pastors of the
> Churches, the Sabbath Schools, Bible Classes, and the Churches
> of our cities and land, should be made the *special* subjects of

prayer for the last half hour each Saturday, that the Sabbath succeeding may be a great day in Zion. The leader will announce the closing hymn punctually five minutes before one—anyone having the floor yielding immediately—and ask for the benediction from any clergyman present. No controverted points discussed or announcements of what denomination the brother may belong to must be made . . . By order of the Committee on Devotional Meetings of the New York Young Men's Christian Association.[24]

Newspapers at the time commented on the need for 'peculiar legislative ability' to lead these meetings.[25] The prominence of businessmen could be both cause and consequence. At the same time, efficiency was seen as a means to an end, and that end was a focus on praying.

It might seem that the stress on 'order' would have meant that there was little spontaneity in these meetings. Some have suggested that there was a sharp distinction in approaches to revival between 'formalists' and 'anti-formalists'.[26] Janice Holmes analyses the influence on the Revival in 1857 and 1858 of a number of Reformed ministers who placed it (she argues) squarely within the context of the 'formalist American revival tradition, one shaped by Calvinists, characterized by a series of national awakenings and sanitized of emotional excesses'.[27] Mark Noll, in his magisterial *America's God*, speaks about the nineteenth-century 'formalists', who, he contends, 'often took center stage in high-profile religious events like the Businessman's Revival'. He contrasts the 'formalist' approach in spirituality with the 'antiformalists' who tended, he suggests, to sectarianism, emotionalism, apocalypticism and conversionism.[28] The contrast, however, should not be overdrawn. Evangelicals have stressed the freedom of the Spirit while at the same time they have not seen this emphasis as implying that everything that truly comes from God is necessarily expressed in the spontaneous and the unstructured. Also, the language of 'formalist' and 'anti-formalist' is somewhat confusing. For Presbyterian ministers in the 1850s in the north of Ireland, for example, 'formalists' were those who lacked an experience of personal conversion.[29]

It is not surprising that many evangelicals within the business world in the northern states of America, who were concerned to see a genuine revival in the churches – and one that was centred on prayer was in their minds genuine – should also see the need for prayer meetings to be properly guided. But the structure adopted and the guidance offered in the meetings were in fact designed to allow a considerable level of participation. Sometimes the leader of the meeting, seeing someone in the audience with information about what was happening in churches elsewhere, would ask for this news to be shared. This kind of specific direction, in which someone in the meeting was invited to speak, was, however, unusual. Normally, after the opening part of the meeting was completed, opportunity was given for anyone to take part, either by offering prayer, or by a short 'exhortation', or by narrating an experience, or by starting a hymn. One limitation to this freedom had to do with women. At the very first of Lanphier's meetings, a woman was turned away. Later, women were part of the meetings but were not invited to play a public part.[30]

An account in Samuel Prime's *The Power of Prayer* gives the atmosphere of one of the prayer meetings in Fulton Street. Prime wrote: 'We take our seat in the middle lecture-room fifteen minutes before twelve, noon. A few ladies are seated in a row of seats in one corner; a few gentlemen are scattered here and there through the room; all is quiet and silent; no talking, no whispering; all has the air of deep solemnity. At ten minutes before twelve, business-men begin to come in rapidly.' A businessman then took his place as chairman. At twelve noon precisely he announced a hymn. Prayer by the leader then followed: 'His prayer is short, exactly to the point; he prays for the Holy Spirit, for the quickening of Christians, for the conversion of sinners here present at this very hour, for the spread of the revival, for the perishing thousands all around us.' After a Bible reading, in this case John chapter 17, prayer requests were read from slips of paper: 'A sister in Massachusetts desires prayer for a brother seventy years of age; a brother, for a sister in Pennsylvania; a mother who has attended these meetings, and thinks she has been benefited, desires prayer for a large family . . .' The meeting was then opened for prayer and prayer was offered, in this case by a clergyman. A hymn followed.[31]

At this point a visitor from St Louis, Missouri, spoke: 'We have heard of this meeting by the mouth of those who have been here with you. We have heard of you through the religious and secular papers, and we have heard from you by means of the telegraph.' He described the 'bond of union' that was felt across the country: 'I cannot tell how we are cheered and encouraged by what we hear from you every week.' The visitor emphasized the 'work of grace' that had been going on, especially among the African American churches in St Louis. After another contribution the leader read from slips of paper that had been passed to the desk as the meeting progressed. These included prayers for churches, and for families, such as: 'Prayer for two brothers, sons of a deceased pastor of one of our Dutch Reformed churches.' Further speakers then described briefly what was going on in their situations, for example, in Philadelphia, at the Jayne's meetings. A man reported that he had presented a request at Fulton Street six weeks previously that God would bless his efforts to establish a prayer meeting at a place in the country to which he was moving. In four weeks, attendance had reached a hundred. Other prayers and testimonies followed, and then the time was up. There was spontaneity, and yet orderliness. A 'brief hour', said Prime, and 'a heavenly place'.[32]

Prayer and catholicity

The unity across denominations to be found in the 1858–59 prayer meetings was also a notable feature. Among the leaders were Baptists, Congregationalists, Episcopalians, Lutherans, Methodists, Presbyterians and members of the Quakers (Society of Friends), as well as those from other groups.

The interdenominational outlook was fostered in North America, but was also seen in other parts of the world. Those affected by the prayer movement began, in turn, to affect all the major denominations. The editor of the *Christian Advocate*, the American Methodist leader Abel Stevens, said in 1858 that the

Revival was 'full of hope' for those seeking greater unity. He continued: 'It shows how easily the great Head of the Church may, when his people shall devote themselves to their essential work, prostrate all walls of partition between them, and bind them forever together in the unity of the Spirit.'[33] Prayer and 'Christian union', as it was termed, were often associated with each other. Prime referred to 'one of the most deeply interesting characteristics of this revival' as its 'catholicity'. The 'union prayer-meeting' was now a known feature of Christian spirituality: one which, he said, 'fills all hearts with joy and gladness'. Prime described how the reality of this union was

> proved from the fact that in all our large towns and cities, the numbers attending upon the union prayer-meetings, far surpassed the numbers attending any one church, or the same place. So it has been in New York. So it has been in Philadelphia, and all our large cities. Thousands go without ever raising the question whom they are to meet, or to what church organisation do they belong. Neither do they care.[34]

Prime may have been a little idealistic about the degree of unity, but he was pinpointing a cross-denominational spirit that was to be an increasing feature in movements of renewal.

Across parts of Ireland by far the strongest support for the Revival was among the Presbyterians, and when there were criticisms of 'emotional revival meetings' the Evangelical Alliance, which had been formed in London in 1846, asked Professor James McCosh, a leading Presbyterian theologian, to write on the subject. McCosh had studied at Edinburgh University under Thomas Chalmers, the great evangelical leader, and after serving as a Free Church of Scotland minister, became Professor of Logic and Metaphysics at Queen's College, Belfast. In October 1859, he published a paper defending the Revival.[35] Although the Presbyterian churches in Ireland gave the lead, other denominations participated, and there were united meetings of Presbyterians, Methodists, Episcopalians, Independents and Baptists. In September 1859, a prayer meeting for the whole of Ireland was arranged in Armagh. Weir wrote in *The Ulster Awakening*:

On Wednesday, 16th September, the second day after I left Armagh, a multitudinous meeting was held there by the friends of the movement in that and in the adjoining counties. In order that a concentrated effort might be made for full attendance, there were special trains from Monaghan, Dungannon, and Belfast. While the crowded train was on its way from Belfast, the sound of voices singing well-known hymns arose from almost every carriage . . . The meeting was held in a capacious field near the Armagh railway station. Very many laymen from England and Scotland were present, as well as clergymen and ministers from different districts of Ireland.[36]

This event, at which twenty thousand people were present, was written up by *The Times*.

By early 1860, in a 'Revival Sermon', C.H. Spurgeon spoke about the way in which – as he saw it – a new spiritual impetus was by then evident across the major denominations in England. United prayer was linked to action. He spoke of the 'life' and 'vigour' being experienced:

Everybody seems to have a mission and everybody is doing it. There may be a great many sluggards, but they do not come across my path now. I used to be always kicking at them, and *always* being kicked for doing so. But now there is nothing to kick *at* – every one is at work – Church of England, Independents, Methodists, and Baptists.[37]

Significantly, Spurgeon *was* looking for more, hoping that through 'God's ploughmen *and* vine dressers' there would be further power – 'that God will bless *us,* and that right early'.[38]

There was great interest in the way *in which* ministers from different denominations were working *togeth*er. A former Anglican clergyman, Baptist W. Noel, who became a Baptist and worked closely with Spurgeon, was one of the *prom*inent speakers at the Armagh meetings in 1859. Spurgeon commented: 'And let me give you another encouragement. Recollect that even when this revival comes, an instrumentality will still be wanted. They began at first to think in the North of Ireland that they could do without ministers, but now that the gospel is spread, never was there such a demand for the preachers of the gospel as now.'[39] Revival involved united prayer and united effort on the part of the churches and their leaders.

The movement that took place in Liverpool from 1859 onwards is a good example of the way in which people from different denominations in England were involved. In the summer of 1859, after Verner M. White, minister of the Presbyterian Church in Islington, Liverpool, had come back from a visit to Ireland, a meeting was held at the instigation of the Liverpool YMCA (Young Men's Christian Association), so that White could give an account of the Revival. The result was that many people in Liverpool were stimulated to pray.[40]

Interdenominational prayer meetings began to take place, with the Liverpool Church of England Scripture Readers' Society commencing a revival prayer meeting. Towards the end of 1859, a united gathering of ministers decided to hold a weekly revival prayer meeting. Large-scale evangelistic meetings also began, for example in the Adelphi Theatre in Liverpool. This phenomenon in major cities will be referred to in more detail in Chapter 7. During 1860, many local congregational prayer meetings took place among all denominations, as well as interdenominational meetings. To give one example of the impact on the churches, of the 11,000 Wesleyan Methodist members on the roll in the Liverpool Circuit in the spring of 1860, 1,800 were new members or probationary members.[41]

The three largest denominations in Scotland were each involved in special prayer meetings. United noon prayer meetings were held, as in North America, and these led to evening prayer meetings in the various churches. The catholic spirit was such that after large interdenominational meetings in 1860 in Perthshire – at one meeting four thousand people were present – those responsible for the meetings stated rather dramatically that they had 'buried sectarianism . . . and saw no Christian weep over its grave'.[42] The General Assembly of the Church of Scotland, held in Edinburgh in May 1860, welcomed 'deepening interest in religious ordinances, followed in many cases by fruits of holy living'. In the same month, the new Moderator of the Free Church of Scotland, James Buchanan, addressed their General Assembly in Edinburgh as follows, 'We, as a Church, accept the Revival as a great and blessed fact. Numerous and explicit testimonies from ministers and members alike bespeak the gracious influence upon the people.' The Synod of the United Presbyterian Church, which was the third largest denomination in Scotland, spoke of 'the hand of God in the measure of new life outpoured upon our churches' and appointed a Sunday in July 1860 as 'a Special Day of Prayer for the Revival'.[43] The Revival was not seen as limited to any one group.

Wales, in the same period, was similar, with a strong emphasis on 'union' prayer meetings. One Welsh minister, writing to Thomas Phillips, who drew together many accounts for his book on the Welsh Revival of 1859, said:

> This is the character of our prayer-meetings both at the church and the chapels. Yes, we hold them in the church, and make it indeed the 'house of prayer' and praise. There is no school-room here large enough for our union prayer-meetings. Clergymen, preachers, and people, pray together, and God is among us. Where there was much bigotry, bickering, and unpleasant feeling between parties before, and had continued for years, there is nothing now but co-operation, love and zeal.[44]

Another correspondent spoke about how the prayer meetings exhibited Christian union and Christian love 'just as Christ commanded'. An old and experienced Welsh Christian, at one of the prayer meetings, prayed in vivid terms: 'O Lord, we thank thee that the straw partition, which has so long separated us, is now on fire!'[45] In the rhythms of revival in this period – and subsequently – there were significant ways in which prayer drew people together.

A concert of prayer

What emerged in the later 1850s and early 1860s, as it had in the previous century, was 'a concert of prayer'. In the eighteenth century, the great North American theologian and preacher, Jonathan Edwards, had proposed the idea of a concert of prayer as an attempt 'to promote agreement and visible union of God's people in prayer for the revival of religion and the advancement of Christ's kingdom'. This was international in its expression. It was taken up in Britain by English Baptists, for instance, John Sutcliff, with his powerful 'Prayer Call' to the Baptist Northamptonshire Association, a call that led to a massive step in the history of world mission with the formation in 1792 of the Baptist Missionary Society.[46]

The call to prayer was given further stimulus in the mid-nineteenth century by a number of factors. One important vehicle for the encouragement of united prayer was the publication in Britain of *The Revival*, edited by R.C. Morgan, a young evangelical who had wide sympathies across the evangelical constituency. This weekly publication had as its stated aim the presentation of information about revivals in North America and Britain. It was seen as serving 'as a record, an advocate, and a stimulus'.[47] Another key factor was the use of the telegraph. Sometimes it was not clear how news spread. One clergyman in Wales, at St David's, Festiniog, simply reported in 1860: 'Hearing at that time [1859] of what was taking place in North America, South Wales, and Ireland, weekly prayer-meetings were held for the outpouring of the Spirit upon us in this neighbourhood.'[48]

As news spread, prayer meetings also spread. In 1859, across England, Scotland, Wales and Ulster, Edwin Orr argues, evangelical Christian communities were affected in every county. He suggests that the evidence he presents indicates that the nineteenth-century movement was as effective nationally as the Evangelical Revival of the previous century.[49] This has been described by Janice Holmes as a 'misjudgement' caused by Orr's reliance on the accounts in *The Revival*. She sees the prayer meetings as preparatory in nature, rather than evidence of revival taking place. In England, she considers, events were rarely to progress beyond this preparatory stage.[50] However, a different view was expressed in *The Baptist Magazine* in 1859. In this issue there was a review of the publications that had been circulating, on both sides of the Atlantic, about the subject of revival. The author of the review wrote

that there was much talk of prayer meetings as 'the instrumental cause of a Revival' but that there was much more to be
said for the opposite view – that the meetings for prayer were
evidence of 'awakened concern' and that when such prayer
took place 'the Revival has already begun'.[51]

The Evangelical Alliance, with its commitment to a broad
vision of evangelical unity, played a crucial role in encouraging a wider understanding of, and concern for, revival. In 1860,
the Evangelical Alliance Council asked Robert Knox, Bishop of
Down, Connor and Dromore, to suggest those who could
speak to English audiences about what had been taking place
in Ulster. Meetings were arranged in eleven venues and
Charles Seaver, the Bishop's nominee, addressed these meetings and also had private conversations with the Archbishop
of Canterbury and the Bishop of London.[52] Unanimity was not
achieved. At one London Alliance meeting William McIlwaine,
a Belfast Presbyterian minister, spoke against the Revival and
was hissed and shouted at by some in the audience. He
expressed his opposition in *Revivalism Reviewed* (1859). This
negative attitude was, however, not typical of those associated
with the Evangelical Alliance.

The first Alliance 'universal week of prayer', in January
1861, came out of a concern for prayer felt in India. In 1860,
North American missionaries in Ludhiana, India, had invited
English-speaking churches to unite in prayer during the second week in January, and one of the missionaries had suggested that in January 1861 the Alliance should send out a
more official call to churches around the world to pray. The
effects of this initiative were far reaching with tens of thousands of copies of a call to prayer being distributed in many
languages for use during the first week in January each year.[53]

The involvement of missionaries in India is an indication of
the way in which the concert of prayer spread around the
world in this period. The global dimension of revival will be
evident in this book. In Sweden there had been spiritual awakening through the ministry of George Scott, a Scottish
Methodist, who had come to Sweden at the invitation of
Samuel Owen, a British industrialist who wanted a spiritual
leader for his English-speaking factory workers. Scott, who

preached in Swedish as well as in English, influenced Karl Olaf Rosenius of Stockholm. Rosenius founded the National Evangelical Foundation in Sweden. News of the 1858 prayer movement in North America and in Britain brought fresh stimulus to prayer meetings in Sweden and the National Evangelical Foundation expanded. Peter Paul Waldenström, who was to succeed Rosenius as a significant leader in Sweden, was converted in 1858 and commenced preaching a year later. Lutheran Church pulpits opened to him.

The movement of prayer and preaching spread from Sweden to Norway, where there was a widespread impact. The Danish island of Bornholm, which is closer to south Sweden than to Denmark, experienced a profound revival in the early 1860s. Germany, too, was affected. A Lutheran pastor from Germany, Theodor Christlieb, served in a Lutheran church in Islington, London, from 1858 to 1865 and was affected by the Revival. He returned to pastoral ministry in Germany where he was a significant figure within the German Evangelical Alliance.[54]

South Africa offers another example of the increasing concert of prayer in this period. In 1860, a revival and mission conference in Worcester in the Cape Province attracted over three hundred South African ministers and missionaries. It was intended to stimulate prayer for spiritual revival and encourage new work by the Dutch Reformed churches of South Africa. News was shared about the recent Revival in North America and Britain and those attending were invited to pray for South Africa. As elsewhere, prayer was central. Andrew Murray had recently become the minister of the Dutch Reformed Church in Worcester. Soon after the conference, a meeting of young people was held at Murray's church and a fifteen-year-old black girl stood up to pray. Other prayers followed and from that evening on daily prayer meetings took place. These began with silence, followed by prayer, which often led to everyone praying together. People right across the community were affected. Andrew Murray tried to quieten the meetings but one evening a visitor gently advised him: 'Be careful what you do, for it is the Spirit of God that is at work here. I have just come from America, and this is precisely what

I witnessed there.' Andrew Murray accepted the advice and became a leader in a movement that spread in many parts of the nation.[55]

The language used by Jonathan Edwards in the eighteenth century – for instance, his reference to 'visible union' in prayer – had clear echoes in the nineteenth century and beyond. Thomas Phillips wrote in 1860 that in prayer together it had been found that 'union is strength'. Many Christian congregations, he said, '[had] united with others for this high and holy purpose [of prayer] in some public room, or alternately in their several places of worship'. Meetings for prayer had been held in

> churches and chapels, in vestries and school-rooms, in town-halls and market-places, in the covered tent and in the open field, in the recesses of the forest and on the mountain top, in the saloons of steamers, and on the open decks of sailing vessels . . . in some instances, elegant drawing-rooms have been thrown open for this purpose, while, on a late memorable occasion, the Egyptian Hall of the Mansion House was converted for the time into a Christian oratory.[56]

Despite the diversity, there was remarkable unity, since 'from the lips and hearts of the thousands who attended them, ONE PRAYER has ascended up before God's throne – "O Lord, revive Thy work in the midst of the years"'. This united prayer, he was confident, had been heard and answered.[57]

Conclusion

The desire to pray, especially with others, which is so evident in this period, is a crucial part of the rhythm of revival. When there is a particular focus on prayer, as there was in many places in the period 1857 to 1863, it is a signal of a revived or reviving Church. Such prayer can be conducted in ways that are orderly without restricting the freedom of the Holy Spirit. The theme of catholicity, of united prayer, is also striking. In this period there was a sense of being part of a global prayer movement. Although the effects of this period of revival were felt for at least a generation, by the beginning of the twentieth century it was a fading memory and there was need of awakening again. Prayer was made and a further wave of revival, an expression of the rhythms of revival, was experienced. This experience was repeated again, at intervals, over the next hundred years. An example of united prayer in recent years has been the 24/7 prayer movement.[58]

Brian Edwards, looking at the theme of prayer in revival and considering especially the later 1850s, notes the earnest prayer and the silent prayer that took place in C.H. Spurgeon's congregation, the estimated ten thousand businessmen praying every day in North America, the prayers made in Ulster for an 'outpouring of the Holy Spirit' and the prayer meetings in 1859 in Wales, which led, as reports put it, to the fact that God was pleased to 'pour down His Spirit from on high, as on the day of Pentecost'. Brian Edwards writes: 'It is not always clear when prayer meetings are part of the revival or are preceding it. But the distinction does not matter too much. Prayer is both the cause and result of the coming of the Spirit in revival.'[59]

3

The Role of Ministers

Because the role of lay people in the rhythms of revival has often been stressed, particularly their key role in the Revival of 1857 onwards, there has at times been a tendency to overlook the part played by the ministers of the various churches that were involved. Yet their participation was crucial. Thomas Phillips wrote in 1860, with reference to Wales:

> What an amount of responsibility now rests upon the ministers of religion of every name! With greater emphasis than ever are they addressed by the great Shepherd, 'Feed my sheep – feed my lambs.' The thousands of additional members may be regarded as children, and as such need to be taught – as recruits, who require to be trained – as newly engaged servants, who must be directed in their work.[1]

Phillips saw the need for ministers to adapt what they were doing in the light of the new situation, although continuing to teach and pastor. His vision was, above all, for ministers to 'train the young converts' so that they would be effective in their own future ministries. In this chapter I will look at the role played by ministers. In Chapter 4 I will examine the complementary role of lay people. There were tensions and at times conflicts between ministers and lay people about issues raised by revival, but it is important to set these tensions in the broader context of commitment to revival on the part of many ministers.

Personal revival

The revival period being examined had a profound effect on many ministers. In North America, one of these ministers was Theodore Cuyler, who graduated from Princeton Seminary in 1846 and after a significant ministry in New Jersey moved to New York, to the Market Street Dutch Reformed Church. He spoke of the joy of this era in his ministry, during which many young men became part of the church, and he highlighted particularly the impact of what he called 'the great revival'. He wrote: 'During the year 1858 occurred the great revival'; and he talked of how 'a mighty wind from Heaven' came upon 'every house where the people of God were sitting'.[2] (By 'house' he referred primarily to congregations.) In 1860, following this intense period, Cuyler was invited by a 'brave little band' (as he later said), 'to a Presbyterian church in Brooklyn which had not had a pastor'. Although he was initially reluctant to move, he came to believe the call was from God. Cuyler took the vision of revival with him and built this church up to 1,600 members, making it the largest Presbyterian congregation in North America at that time. The year 1866 saw a significant revival in the Brooklyn church, as a result of which 320 people were added to the church membership in this year alone.[3] Reviewing his life, Cuyler spoke of disappointments, yet also of the mysterious way in which 'several copious showers of heavenly blessing have descended when we were not expecting them'.[4] Ministers such as Cuyler, who were affected by revival, often had a significant continuing impact.

As one of the leading figures in the Revival in Wales, David Morgan gave attention to the responsibilities of the pastors for their own spiritual renewal. He suggested that there were certain priorities for those who preached and taught. The first necessity, for him, was 'to pray much in secret – to be there many times in the day, wrestling with God – to wrestle each time as if it were the last, and not to rise from your knees until you have a proof that the Lord has heard you. Ask the Lord in faith, and with great fervency, what to say to the people'. This was about the preacher's inner life. If the life of prayer was given priority by ministers, then, Morgan believed, 'will the anointing follow your preaching'. He also advised preachers to be 'pointed' in their application of their message to their hearers and to preach in a rousing way.[5] Another Welsh minister in this period spoke warmly about how the Revival had brought about great changes not only in 'the style of preaching' but also 'in the spirit of the preacher'. Many congregations in Wales felt that preachers and people 'had been brought together into close contact'.[6]

In the north-east of Scotland there was concern in 1859 that the churches were losing touch with young people working on the farms in Aberdeenshire. To investigate what should be done, the Aberdeen Free Church Synod set up a committee chaired by Robert Reid, minister of Banchory Ternan Free Church. The committee recommended that reaching young people should be a priority. However, the recommendations of a committee were not sufficient to achieve the desired result. According to one minister, William Dower, the influence of Reid himself was crucial. Banchory, a community on the river Dee, inland from Aberdeen, became a centre of revival from May 1859, and the movement in the town spread to other places. Dower wrote that Reid 'became the inspiration of the revival movement from the city as far west as Braemar', and added that through Reid 'the village of Banchory Ternan became a kind of transmitting centre to the regions beyond and the parishes around'. Kenneth Jeffrey speaks of Reid and three other Free Church ministers as 'the spiritual directors of the movement', Reid, then aged forty-eight, being the oldest member of this group.[7] The spiritual renewal to which ministers such as Reid were committed had a profound impact.

David Adams, describing what happened at Ahoghill in Ulster (he was the minister of the First Presbyterian Church in Ahoghill), argued that the Revival 'did not come so suddenly and unexpectedly as some imagine'. From his ordination as a Presbyterian minister in 1841, Adams had felt an intense desire for what he termed 'such a time of refreshing', and had repeatedly preached to his own congregation, and also on public occasions, about 'the outpouring of the Spirit'. He had also undertaken pastoral visitation from house to house in the parish so that he could follow up the concerns expressed in his preaching from the pulpit. Two sermons by Adams, on 'Pentecost', and on 'The Conversion of the Apostle Paul', were, it seems, particularly effective. Even before the Revival, the congregations were increasing and the decision was made to erect a new and larger church building. It was opened in 1858, and Adams later said:

> I regard it as a singular token of God's good providence, that it was just ready for the great Revival harvest. If it had not been so, hundreds of devout inquirers after the truth could not have obtained accommodation. Some of our people thought it folly to attempt building such a large, handsome place of worship, but the Lord, notwithstanding, graciously led us in the right way, as all now thankfully admit.[8]

C.H. Spurgeon, in his extensive work of training ministers (in 1892, the year of Spurgeon's death, his college had trained nearly nine hundred students for the ministry), placed great emphasis on the spiritual life of the pastor, encouraging ministers to make spirituality central to their pastoral work. On many occasions in the 1860s he addressed this issue, for example, in his magazine, *The Sword and the Trowel*, which was read by many ministers, not only from the Baptist Union, but also from other denominations. 'It is very hard work to preach when the head aches and when the body is languid,' he stated, no doubt referring to his own ill health, 'but it is a much harder task when the soul is unfeeling and lifeless.' Spurgeon believed that the saddest experience of all was when ministers did not actually feel it to be sad that they (or, as he said, 'we') could 'go on preaching and remain careless concerning the truths we preach'. He spoke of some ministers who acted merely as signposts, pointing out the road along which people should travel but never moving along it themselves.[9] Spurgeon believed there were important consequences when ministers were themselves spiritually revived.

Caring for the people

Commitment to pastoral care in times of revival is very well illustrated in the case of a well-known Baptist pastor in North America, Francis Wayland, who was President of Brown University for twenty-eight years and in 1857 became pastor of the First Baptist Church in Providence, Rhode Island. Wayland's correspondence, later published by his sons, indicates that he began to be aware at the beginning of 1858 that his energy was lessening (he was then in his early sixties) but when he became conscious of 'a spirit of revival' he began to visit energetically around his area. If he heard of 'a case of inquiry or interest' he at once set out to talk to the enquirer. He walked rather than rode on horseback and spoke to 'acquaintances on the street, or in shops'. One member of Wayland's family described walking with Wayland down the street when Wayland said: 'There is a man who has been avoiding me for weeks. I want to speak to him.' Another person, a young women, 'was quite determined that he [Wayland] should not move her, nor even speak to her on religion, if she could avoid it'. However, when Wayland met her the opposition melted away, and she experienced a complete spiritual change.[10]

The efforts of a Baptist pastor in New Hampshire (noted by Kathryn Long) were typical of the involvement of many ministers in caring for people during the period of revival. This minister, who signed himself J.K.C., wrote in 1858 to the *Watchman and Reflector* outlining his experiences. He reported: 'In going from house to house the writer found several persons serious.' He spoke about the work progressing until twenty-five people had been 'hopefully converted'.[11]

Pastoral care by ministers was also a marked feature in the north of Ireland. John Weir, in his book on the 'Ulster Awakening', quoted a minister in Belfast who spoke about 'the overwhelming fatigue' that he and other ministers were feeling as a result of visiting, speaking to and praying with so many people who had been affected by the Revival. Several ministers, he said, were often involved until two or three o'clock in the morning. This minister said that only late on a Saturday evening could he find a little time for preparation for the Sunday services. Weir commented that many ministers almost envied the 'weariness' of their Belfast brothers.[12]

Often concern for people's spiritual needs led to extended meetings, for example, at Berry Street Presbyterian Church in Belfast, where the popular Hugh Hanna was minister. Hanna was one of a growing number of ministers in the 1850s who engaged in open-air preaching, a practice that was somewhat controversial in Presbyterian circles.[13] William Gibson, who wrote *The Year of Grace*, was invited to speak at Berry Street and gave a short address on 'the unconditional freeness of the gospel offer'. Gibson wanted, as he put it, 'to repress any tendency to mere excitement', and he spoke in 'the most didactic and unimpassioned strain'. Nonetheless, there was deep emotion in the meeting. Those overwhelmed by their feelings were guided out of the meeting and the service proceeded to its 'close', but, added Gibson, 'After the benediction the congregation kept their seats, and showed no disposition to retire. It was necessary, therefore, to resume, and again address the thirsting multitude. The benediction was a second time pronounced, and yet they lingered in the sanctuary.'[14]

While Gibson and many of his fellow Presbyterians threw themselves into the work of the Revival, seeing it as a period of God's grace, others wrote against it. One minister, Isaac Nelson, a Presbyterian who was later a Member of Parliament, rather bitterly labelled the Revival period a 'year of delusion',[15] not (as Gibson termed it) a 'year of grace', and there were suggestions in several quarters that extended meetings resulted in bizarre behaviour. It seems that in some cases lay people in Ulster were more committed than ministers to the extension of revival meetings beyond their normal times. Thus Thomas Watters of Newtownards stated that meetings in his church should end at 10.00 p.m. But at one meeting John Colville, an elder, got up to pray and included in his prayer the words, 'If the clock strikes ten, let it strike ten', and he then continued by making it clear that in his view the people should not be influenced by clocks. However, it is possible to overstate tensions between ministers and lay people over such issues. It is not so much that the ministers feared a loss of authority (as is sometimes argued), but rather that – at least in many cases – they had a genuine concern for the welfare of the people and were seeking to bring pastoral wisdom to bear on the new outburst of spiritual energy.[16]

Although the ministers who were most deeply involved in the encouragement of the Revival in the north of Ireland were Presbyterians, oversight of the movement was also provided from within the Episcopal Church. Bishop Robert Knox, for example, invited all the clergy in his dioceses to a breakfast to discuss how to give appropriate pastoral guidance within the context of the emotion and phenomena that accompanied revival. Although there were serious reservations about the phenomena, all of those present agreed that the Revival was a work of God. The incumbent of Trinity Episcopal Church, Belfast, Theophilus Campbell, an advocate of the Revival, said that in the case of most of those who professed conversion the emotions shown were natural – tears and some shaking. Campbell saw the fruit of the movement as being evident in many changed lives in his parish.[17] When, in 1860, Knox asked his clergy for their assessment of the effect of the Revival in their parishes, out of about 70 parishes, 51 reported on a marked improvement in spiritual life and attendance at services. In the remainder, the clergy generally reported some improvement, while a few said there had been no change.[18]

Similar pastoral care was exercised by many evangelical ministers in Scotland. Again, it is possible to show that there were occasional tensions between lay people and ministers, but on the whole, pastoral oversight was exercised by ministers in such a way as to foster the Revival. During the first week of September 1859, for example, the Free Church of Scotland Synod of Argyll, in the west of Scotland, met at Campbeltown and at an evening meeting a number of those present who had been to Ireland gave an account of 'the work of God' as they had seen it there. This generated considerable interest. Three weeks later the largest church in Campbeltown (the Gaelic-speaking Free Church, seating 1,700) began to be opened for prayer each evening and was full to overflowing. It was reckoned that four thousand people out of a total population of nine thousand were at prayer meetings. The twenty local pubs found that they were much less sought after than the prayer meetings. In another town in Argyll, Inverary, the ministers, Gilbert Meikle and Robert Rose, were active in giving people spiritual guidance. One of the converts of the Revival there was James Chalmers, later a famous pioneer missionary in New Guinea. Chalmers was initially intent on disrupting the meetings but was impressed by what he heard from two Irish speakers who had been affected by the Revival and he received spiritual guidance from Meikle. Ministers across Scotland played an active part in guiding what happened in the revivals in this period.[19]

Impact on preaching

Within the rhythms of revival, there are specific features that mark certain contexts but there are also observable constants. One of these is the ministry of the word. In North America, well-established ministers found that their preaching took on new power. Francis Wayland is a classic example. His biographers (his sons) noted: 'Meanwhile, Dr. Wayland's sermons became even more direct than before, – more affectionate and solemn. He gradually relinquished the practice of writing his discourses.' At mid-week meetings 'he spoke as he had never done before'. His direct preaching was welcomed by his congregation. From the moment that he stood up to begin a service there was a powerful sense among the people of the immediate presence of God. 'We have come to meet *thee*' was an expression Wayland almost always used in prayer. His biographers record that 'every heart expected to hold communion with Christ'. The meetings were also opened for response. One evening, a person 'who had been a backslider for twenty years, was speaking of his wandering, and of his repentance'. As Wayland listened to this testimony, he was overcome with emotion and some moments passed before he was able to continue to lead the service.[20]

Very experienced preachers found that their preaching entered into new dimensions. The content of what they said was largely the same, but it was said in new ways. This factor is exemplified well in a report written on 29 February 1860 by

D.C. Jones, a minister in Abergwili, in Carmarthenshire, about revival in his area of Wales. He wrote: 'We have been visited with a larger measure of the Spirit's influences than usual. It came suddenly "like a rushing mighty wind", and that apparently when the churches little expected it.' More details then followed: 'The first indications were observed in the month of May last, when the prayer-meetings were better attended, and larger numbers came to the public services on the Lord's day, and more punctually than usual.' (It is perhaps encouraging to observe that lateness is not a product of a particular culture or a particular time in history!) What is significant is that Jones found that his regular preaching was received with greater attentiveness. 'It was evident', he continued, 'from the earnest attention paid to the sermons and to every part of the service, that a deep feeling pervaded the congregation. I endeavoured to deepen and to draw out this earnest feeling by preaching from Hosea xiii. 13. This was done in my two congregations and with marked effect.' All of this yielded fruit. During the three succeeding months, Jones gave 'the right hand of fellowship' (a sign of welcome into church membership) to more than two hundred people.[21]

William Gibson included in his *The Year of Grace* many examples of the effect of preaching in the north of Ireland. Like Thomas Phillips in Wales, Gibson's approach was to gather details from a wide range of ministers. One of these was William Johnston of Townsend Street Presbyterian Church, Belfast, a congregation established in 1833. Johnston described at length how across his congregation a number of people had, as he put it, received the 'baptism of the Holy Spirit'. He spoke of the effect of both preaching and prayer, and of how these related to each other. He highlighted a conversation with one of his elders, John, who was to accompany him on pastoral visiting. This conversation had taken place part way through the period of intense experience of revival. Johnston wrote: 'When seated together at his [John's] fireside, he said, "I think, Mr Johnston, the ministers are all *preaching* a great deal better than they used to do."' The reply from the minister was that it might be the case that 'the people are *hearing* a good deal better than they used to do'. John, not be out-done in the conversation, suggested that 'they *ought* to preach a good deal better' because 'the people are all praying now for their ministers; and before this revival, they left all the praying as well as the preaching to them'.[22]

Effective preaching by local church pastors, some of whom had a wider ministry, was also prominent in many other places where revival was evident. Edwin Orr speaks about 'empowered preachers'. His analysis would have been more helpful if he had distinguished between ministers of congregations and itinerant evangelists, since they often carried out different functions.[23] Some ministers, however, did have both a local and a wider role. C.H. Spurgeon was a leading example of a minister whose wider influence was immense. In January 1860, with the powerful impact of revival still being felt, Spurgeon preached five times to capacity audiences at the Metropolitan Hall in Dublin (later Merrion Hall), which seated about three thousand people. Later in the same year, in August, *The Revival* reported on the effect of the preaching taking place in one local church in Glasgow:

> Every Sabbath evening service since the Bridgetown Church was opened, the crowds around the stone [open air] pulpit have been increasing, until on Sabbath evening last, there could not have been fewer than seven thousand hearers, probably more. We say 'hearers', for, notwithstanding the vastness of the congregation, the voice of the preacher appeared to be perfectly audible at the further extremity.[24]

A prayer meeting inside the church, at which there were over a thousand people, followed the open-air preaching service, and those who wished after that to have conversation with the minister of the church or with lay leaders remained behind. About five hundred did so on the occasion to which the report referred. It is significant that although the preaching was clearly central, the name of the preacher is not mentioned.

The same stress on the power of the ministry of the word, but without a 'powerful personality', was to be found in England. Handley Moule, who became a leading evangelical scholar and then Bishop of Durham, recalled his impression of what happened in rural Dorset. Moule and Evan Hopkins – both of whom were to become Keswick leaders – were among those affected. Moule, writing of 'one wonderful epoch in the parish [of Fordington]', says:

> It was the Revival. The year was 1859, that 'year of the right hand of the Most High' . . . Ulster was profoundly and lastingly moved and blessed. Here and there in England it was the same: and Fordington was one of the scenes of Divine Awakening. For surely it was Divine. No artificial means of excitement were dreamt of . . . No powerful personality, no Moody or Aitken, came to us . . . Up and down the village the pastor, the pastoress and their faithful helpers found 'the anxious'. And the church was thronged to overflowing.

The 'pastor and pastoress' (a striking combination) were Moule's parents. His father, Henry, the vicar, had been a solicitor and banker. His ministry in Fordington included a period, in 1854, when the parish had to deal with a terrible cholera epidemic. Moule visited the sick, organized what was a very poor community to defend itself, lobbied for help, and in all this saved many lives. Handley Moule estimated that five years after this hundreds of people were spiritually awakened, with the church 'thronged to overflowing' night after night as the reading and preaching of scripture 'carried with them a heavenly power'.[25] Among those affected was Thomas Hardy, later the famous novelist, who at the time was a friend of Horace Moule, Handley's oldest brother. Hardy's commitment to evangelical Christianity did not, however, survive after his move to London in 1862.[26]

The Fordington Revival was unusual in being largely among the very poor, and C.H. Spurgeon, who was a close observer of the effects of revival, had an on-going concern that not enough attention was being paid by local congregations and their ministers to communicating with working-class people. Although working-class evangelists were successful (I will look at this in the next chapter), there were ministers whose approach was far removed from the needs of people who might have been drawn into the churches. In

1863, Spurgeon pronounced gloomily: 'Ten years ago we could speak honestly that the Churches were almost dead, but I think they are worse now, because they have cherished the idea that they are not so dead as they were.'[27] Spurgeon was given to mood swings, and his comment should be interpreted with that in mind, but he clearly had a particular anxiety about the type of preaching that was gaining ground in the post-Revival period. 'The language of half our pulpits', Spurgeon argued in 1870, 'is alienating the working classes from public worship', and in typically blunt style he stated: 'Now the devil does not care for your dialectics, and eclectic homiletics, or Germanic objectives and subjectives; but pelt him with Anglo-Saxon in the name of God, and he will shift his quarters.'[28] In some circles there was a cultivation of 'high-brow' preaching. Spurgeon saw the function of preaching very differently. His commitment was to the kind of direct, accessible preaching that had been widely observable in the period of revival in the later 1850s and early 1860s.

The phenomena of revival

It is not, however, that Spurgeon was uncritical of the Revival preaching. Indeed, his criticisms became more pointed as time went on. Although he saw much in the movement that he applauded, in October 1859 – when making reference to his own ministry and to the revival he believed he had experienced – he felt the need at the same time to issue a veiled warning about the phenomena that were becoming evident in some places, espec-ially in the north of Ireland. Speaking of his own church, Spurgeon said:

> These five years or more we have had a revival which is not to be exceeded by any revival upon the face of the earth. Without cries or shoutings, without fallings down or swooning, steadily God adds to this church numbers upon numbers, so that your minister's heart is ready to break with very joy when he thinks how manifestly the Spirit of God is with us.'[29]

In making reference to 'cries and shoutings', and 'fallings down or swooning', Spurgeon was taking up a topic that was being much debated not only in Christian circles but also more widely. *The Lancet*, the leading medical journal, had an article in July 1859 entitled, 'The physical phenomena of revival', in which the physical manifestations that were to be found in Ireland were dismissed as 'hysteria', and as 'morbid and injurious'.[30]

How did the ministers in the north of Ireland react to these phenomena? Adam Magill, minister in Boveva, wrote of dramatic occurrences in his church:

> A large number of my congregation were stricken to the earth, as if suddenly pierced with a spear, whilst others were distressed and perplexed with an awful sense of un-worthiness. The *effects* in both cases were similar, being manifested in the earnest, prayerful devotedness of their lives, teaching us to submit to whatever way the Spirit of the Lord may please to work.[31]

Magill felt that he should 'venture an opinion on the bodily distress many endured' and suggested that this came from 'a sense of guilt pressing on the mind'. He also argued that in a situation where so many people had become 'gospel-hardened' and resistant to preaching, 'God saw that an extraordinary remedy was necessary'. Thus for Magill the physical manifestations – being 'struck', and the cries for mercy – were designed by God to be messages 'preached with greater power to a careless people than the most eloquent sermon that could be delivered'. As he sought to discern what was happening with the 'physical features of the revival' he said that he felt constrained to bow and say: 'It is the Lord, let him do as it seemeth him good.'[32]

A rather more cautious note was sounded by James McCosh in his article, 'The Ulster Revival and Its Physiological Accidents', which appeared in the October edition of the Evangelical Alliance's *Evangelical Christendom*.[33] In it, he argued – as did other Presbyterian ministers at the time – that the prostrations, trembling and other dramatic phenomena associated with the Revival could function as marks of the

Holy Spirit's work; but they required to be verified by the changed moral and spiritual character of those who experienced them. Another minister, Richard Smith, in Derry, spoke of 'prostration' and 'visions' among people in his congregation, highlighting one young woman who had experienced powerful visions and 'continues steadfast in the faith of Jesus, and is an example of humility and love, and all the other graces of the Spirit'. Smith stressed that such experiences were 'comparatively few'. He did not dismiss them, however. In the case of the young woman, she never spoke later about her experiences, nor did Smith encourage her to speak for, he said, 'I knew her mind to have been strung to an ecstatic pitch.' Smith was not aware of one single 'stricken' case in Derry that turned out to be spurious.[34] McCosh, whose positive assessment was widely circulated through the Evangelical Alliance, moved from Belfast to Princeton College, USA, in 1868, and his continuing interest in analysing religious experience and belief led him to deliver a series of lectures, later published as *Christianity and Positivism*.[35]

Thomas Phillips, writing in 1860 about what was happening in the Revival in Wales with regard to extraordinary occurrences, said: 'I am not aware that men, women and children are "struck", as in Ireland; but multitudes, of all ages, are so pierced to the heart by convictions as to produce emotions strong and deep and overpowering.' He and others who corresponded with him spoke of 'loud weeping, as well as subdued sobbing', of 'strong cries' as well as – in typically Welsh fashion – 'rejoicing of soul, expressed in impassioned singing, and long-continued, and oft-repeated hallelujahs of praise'.[36] After one Saturday morning meeting in Carmarthenshire, where the effects of the Revival were regarded as particularly powerful, those who had recently been converted went to a nearby field where they were 'overpowered by the Spirit of God' and poured out their hearts in praise. Some shouted, 'Blessed be the name of God for thus remembering us in mercy.' Before long hundreds of people came together and, an observer recorded, 'The Spirit of God descended upon them in a wondrous manner, till all testified that God was really in that place.'[37]

There was an acceptance by those involved in the Revival that meetings were not ultimately under human control. John L. Girardeau, a Presbyterian minister in Charleston, South Carolina, USA, who described the Revival of the late 1850s as the greatest event of his life, recounted how at one prayer meeting he received a strange physical feeling as if (wrote his biographer), 'a bolt of electricity had struck his head and diffused itself through his whole body'. His ministry was among the African American slave community and he built up a congregation from 36 members to 600, with 1,500 attending. The church was known for its preaching – Girardeau was called 'the Spurgeon of America' – and its social ministry. During the period of revival, however, Girardeau emphasized prayer. When he felt the 'bolt of electricity', he said: 'The Holy Spirit has come; we will begin preaching tomorrow evening.' Girardeau closed the service with a hymn, dismissed the congregation, and came down from the pulpit; but no one left. Instead they began to sob, first softly, and then, with deeper emotion, to weep or to rejoice. It was midnight before he could dismiss his congregation. A noted evangelist from the north who was present said, 'I never saw it on this fashion.' The meetings went on virtually night and day for eight weeks. Within a social context of segregation, large numbers of both black and white people were converted. His own congregation was built up, not only in numbers, but also in spiritual experience, a factor that remained a powerful element in the church.[38]

In May 1860, C.H. Spurgeon was more explicit in his criticisms of strange experiences in revival, speaking about certain Christians in London who had fallen into the error of 'wanting to see signs and wonders'. Some people, he said,

> [had been] meeting together in special prayer-meetings to seek for a revival; and because people have not dropped down in a fainting fit, and have not screamed and made a noise, perhaps they have thought the revival has not come. Oh that we had but eyes to see God's gifts in the way God chooses to give them! We do not want the revival of the North of Ireland, we want the revival in its goodness, but not in that particular shape.[39]

Spurgeon followed this with remarks in the following year about the North American Revival as a 'great wave and then dry sand' and expressed his fear that what had happened in Ireland would come to the same end. 'The fact is,' said Spurgeon, 'the Church is not healthy; she has intermittent fits of health.'[40] It seems, however, that Spurgeon was being unduly pessimistic. An Evangelical Alliance report in 1860 spoke of the main effects in Ulster: full preaching services, more people than ever at services of Holy Communion, many more prayer meetings, increased family prayer and Bible reading, growth among Sunday schools, consistent lives among converts, increased giving, and a reduction in crime.[41] This was the picture that was, generally speaking, conveyed by ministers who were involved in communities affected by revival.

Training others

In this period of revival, ministers affected by revival in very different geographical contexts were concerned to see a younger generation trained for ministry – an important rhythm of revival. In Wales, one of the centres of training was Trevecca College in south Wales, which had been built in the eighteenth century by Selina, Countess of Huntingdon, on the site of an old castle. It was still regarded as a 'school of the prophets' in the 1850s. In the winter of 1857, there was a significant time at the College. David Charles, President of the College, described it in this way:

> An unusual spirit had possessed the students and the little church at this place for some time. You know that we are accustomed to hold weekly church-meetings in Wales, at which members relate the different dealings of God with their souls, when exhortations, warnings, and directions are given, suitable to the occasion, and the great truths of revelation are treated in their relation to living faith and practice. These our church-meetings had become as little Bethels to us for some months. The testimony of our consciences after each successive meeting was that God was there.[42]

One of the students added his perspective: 'It has recently been our good fortune to be favoured with occasions of spiritual delight and blessing, and we cannot do other than rejoice at recalling and relating such glorious circumstances, which have been, in truth, a refreshing to our souls'.[43]

The situation was similar in other Welsh colleges. In the Independent (Congregational) College in Brecon, for instance, the students were also stirred up. David Rowlands, a student who subsequently became Principal at Brecon, acknowledged his debt to the Revival. William Griffiths, a Congregational preacher, reported that tutors as well as students were 'full of the revival fire'.[44] In 1859, the staff and many of the students at the Theological College in Bala were powerfully moved by the ministries of Thomas Edwards of Penllwyn and David Morgan; the Principal, Lewis Edwards, was also supportive. Thomas Charles Edwards from Bala, a theological student in Oxford, described what had happened in Bala and gave his own testimony:

> I was in College at the time studying great matters, but never having realised them in my experience as living truths . . . But here came two plain men from Cardiganshire to Bala, and preached Jesus Christ simply and unaffectedly, without much culture or eloquence: but they had more . . . no one needed Butler's arguments or Paley's evidence. The change that I experienced was ample evidence to me of the Divinity of Christianity.[45]

Edwards was to become the first Principal of the University College of Wales, Aberystwyth, and then for a brief period Principal of Bala Theological College. He showed how to integrate theological argument and experience.

There was a significant impact on theological students in the north of Ireland. The numbers in training for Presbyterian ministry increased from 64 in 1858 to 125 in 1861, and continued to increase. While some students were wary of aspects of the Revival – one, J.B. Armour, spoke of the use of the penitent's form in a Presbyterian church as 'very far from right'[46] – but William Gibson wrote: 'Among those engaged, in the course of the summer of 1859, in the advancement of the work of God, were many young men in course of preparation for the ministry. A goodly number of these were themselves quickened into newness of life, and willingly consecrated their energies to the holy cause.' Their dedication to the work of the Revival had an effect on their studies. Gibson noted that 'when the period arrived for the bestowal of the degrees and other literary and scientific honours, annually awarded by Queen's University, several of the undergraduates were found to have withdrawn for the time from the competition'. This was noted publically by the Vice-Chancellor of the University, although in reporting this Gibson did not comment on the view of the Vice-Chancellor. Gibson's own perspective was not in doubt: for him, the experience the students acquired within the few months in which they were involved in the movement of awakening 'gave them a profounder insight into the mode of dealing with individual souls than they could have attained by whole years of academic training'.[47]

Training within the Anglican world was also affected in this period. Two significant developments took place in 1860. Revival in the area of Barnet, north of London, was embraced by William Pennefather, who was then the incumbent of Christ Church, Barnet. In the same year, Pennefather launched the deaconess movement, in which young women were trained for service in the Anglican Church, and uniformed deaconesses began to work in many evangelical Anglican parishes. In 1864, Pennefather moved to St Jude's, Mildmay Park, where he became known as the leader of the Mildmay Conferences.

Another development in 1860 was that T.P. Boultbee, an Anglican evangelical scholar who was a Fellow of St John's College, Cambridge, urged fellow Anglican evangelicals to set up an evangelical theological college. St Aidan's, Birkenhead, already existed, but it was a significant step forward for Anglican evangelicals when, in 1863, a college was opened in the London area. It began in St John's Hall, Highbury, with Boultbee as Principal, and soon went from one initial student to fifty and then sixty students. Alfred Peache and his sister were the main financial backers of the College. There were links with Mildmay, and in 1865 Charles Waller, a curate at

Mildmay Park, became a tutor at St John's. When Waller retired in 1898, St John's (or the London College of Divinity, as it became) had trained over seven hundred students, most of them for the Anglican ministry.[48] The Revival gave impetus to new initiatives in the training of clergy.

A Free Church equivalent of St John's was the Pastors' College, founded by C.H. Spurgeon in 1856. Like St John's, it began with one student and grew rapidly. At the time of Spurgeon's death in 1892, the number of students who had been trained at the Pastors' College (the name was changed to Spurgeon's College in 1923) numbered 863, and 627 of them were serving in the Baptist denomination as pastors, missionaries and evangelists. More than ninety thousand people had been baptized in churches led by former students of the College. Over half the new churches founded within the Baptist denomination in the period 1865 to 1887 were as a result of the activities of Spurgeon and the students of the College.[49]

It was a regular complaint in Spurgeonic circles that there was too much stress on academic scholarship in the training offered for the ministry in other colleges. 'Collegiate training', George Rogers (the first Principal of the Pastors' College) noted in 1866, 'had hitherto been limited to a particular class of candidates, and to a particular kind and amount of education.' Rogers asked if students trained in this way were known to have more impact as ministers and he answered with a resounding 'No!' It was against this background that the College had developed in the late 1850s and early 1860s – the period of the Revival – a 'new method of collegiate training, better adapted to the real wants of the age'.[50] What the College aimed at, Spurgeon stated in 1870, was not to reach people of 'high culture' but to be relevant to the needs of the majority of the population, which required ministers marked by 'vital godliness'.[51]

Conclusion

In the many books that have been written on revival, the dimensions of ministerial involvement in the rhythms of revival, though covered, have often not been given particular emphasis. Attention has been directed to preaching, to the role of travelling evangelists and the work of lay people generally. The ways in which those other than ministers contribute to revivals are crucial and will be looked at in the next chapter. It is significant, however, that when Brian Edwards listed the names of those whom God had used, the majority were ordained ministers of various denominations.[52]

In the period 1857 to 1863 ministers contributed to the Revival by their personal engagement. It was not that having a minister whose own spiritual experience was revived was a formula for wider revival. Indeed, it was not uncommon for ministers themselves to be challenged by the movement of renewal. But their attitude was often crucial. When they became fully involved in the new movement, through pastoral care and preaching, renewal was likely to develop in healthy ways. Their discernment was also significant when it came to unusual phenomena, although – as has often been the case – ministers were not agreed among themselves as to the spiritual authenticity or desirability of such phenomena. Humphrey Jones, who was an early supporter of the Revival in America and a pioneer in Wales, later attempted to prohibit preaching in revival meetings and engaged in bizarre prophecy. Ministers were not able to manufacture genuine revival, but they had a responsibility for the shape it took. Many ministers were also involved, with others, in seeking to encourage a new generation – including theological students – to embrace dynamic spiritual experience as integral to the outworking of their faith.

4

Emerging Evangelists

'The emergence of leaders in Great Britain', says Edwin Orr, 'was a distinct feature of the British Awakening in the 1860s.' He contrasts this with the North American Revival, which he calls a 'spontaneous, leaderless turning to God'.[1] The situation in different parts of Britain, however, as Orr acknowledges, was varied. In the north of Ireland and in Wales, there were a few leaders who travelled around the various parts of the country giving what might be termed spiritual direction. David Morgan in part fulfilled that role in Wales, since he was not a minister of a congregation and was free to travel. In Scotland, a number of evangelists participated in the Revival and then moved south to continue their work by travelling around in England. It was principally in England, followed by southern Ireland, that what Orr calls 'emerging evangelists' (a term that for him includes workers in, and converts of the first period of the Revival) 'accomplished the main evangelistic mission of the Awakening'.[2]

In this chapter I will look at the role of the varied evangelistic leaders of the Revival of this period, some of whom were ministers who engaged in travelling ministries, but most of whom were lay leaders. I will include particular consideration of the emergence of women as significant leaders. It is clear that as well as the local church pastors (who were the subject of Chapter 3), a number of men and women who were not ordained were at the heart of the rhythms of revival of the later 1850s and thereafter.

International evangelists

A few travelling evangelists were active before 1857 and made their own contribution to the Revival when it was under way. The most famous names in this group are probably Charles Finney and James Caughey, and much has been written about them.[3] I am going to give attention here, however, to those who 'emerged' as significant international figures in this mid-century period. They did not create the Revival, but they contributed to its development and their own ministries grew as a result of it. Henry Grattan Guinness, who was born in Dun Laoghaire (then Kingstown), near Dublin, in 1835, and was from a brewing family, was probably the foremost among the British evangelists involved in the Revival, and his ministry took on important international dimensions. Another powerful international figure was William Taylor, a Methodist who, in the 1850s – when working in many parts of California (beginning in San Francisco) during the Gold Rush – was well known as the Californian 'street preacher'. After the Revival he began to feel a call to worldwide ministry. Finally, I want to look at the international ministry of Walter and Phoebe Palmer, who were involved in revival meetings in Canada – in Ontario and Quebec – in autumn 1857.

Grattan Guinness was a globetrotter by nature, but when he was converted to Christ at the age of twenty his desire for adventure was redirected so that rather than simply seeking to enjoy himself, he became involved in helping others. Guinness addressed huge crowds and saw a remarkable response. He was reckoned to be the most popular preacher in the north of Ireland during the Revival period; on one occasion he addressed twenty thousand people from the top of a cab. Recalling this period fifty years later, he wrote that 'the predominating feature was the conversion of people of all ranks and positions, in ways sudden, startling, amazing'. He had seen people converted in small numbers before, but found the response in 1859 to be a completely new experience. The message had not changed, but in terms of the rhythms of spiritual life something new was happening. Later, Guinness sought to mobilize for world mission those affected by the Revival. This led in the 1870s to the launch of the East London Training Institute (afterwards Harley College), through which Grattan and his wife Fanny trained well over a thousand missionaries from thirty denominations, and also to the formation of the Livingstone Inland Mission (with echoes of Hudson Taylor's China Inland Mission) to the Congo. Guinness also founded what became the Regions Beyond Missionary Union. F.B. Meyer and C.H. Spurgeon were among the leading Baptist ministers who admired and supported Guinness' work.[4]

William Taylor had been converted in 1841 (like Guinness, when he was twenty) at a camp meeting. Initially he worked for the Methodist Episcopal Church in Baltimore, but had seven years in California as a self-supporting missionary (a position he advocated), concentrating on the needs of Chinese immigrants and on the poor. He then moved from California back to the eastern states of America and was involved in and affected by the 1857–58 Revival in the United States and Canada.[5] After sensing a call to international ministry, he moved to Australia in 1863. All the denominations in Australia saw significant growth in the period from 1857 to 1864 but the growth among Methodists, among whom Taylor worked, was the most dramatic. Taylor moved from Australia to South Africa, where he was dismayed by the small Methodist congregations he found. He preached to Xhosa congregations on 'receiving power' when the Holy Spirit comes, and in the coming months many thousands professed conversion. Taylor spoke of the power of the Spirit in the meetings as greater than he had ever experienced. The Xhosa people gave him the name 'Isikuni Sivutayo', the 'Blazing Firebrand'. When he left Australia Taylor claimed that six thousand conversions had taken place over two and a half years, and when he left southern Africa he spoke of eight thousand converts, the vast majority African.[6]

In thinking about rhythms of revival, it is important to note that the effects of Taylor's ministry were long lasting. In South Africa, Wesleyan Home Mission Bands were formed as a result of the awakening of the 1860s and these had an effective ministry into the twentieth century. When Taylor was preaching to the Xhosa congregations, his translator was Charles

Pamla, a young African chief who was a superbly gifted communicator. Pamla became a preacher all across South Africa and when he died it was reckoned that twenty-five thousand had come to know Christ through his ministry. Methodist Home Mission was also very effective among Bantu people. Taylor had made an enormous impact among Bantu tribesmen, with one report at the time seeing his ministry as marking a new stage after half a century of Methodist mission in South Africa. This proved to be the case. Methodism became the leading movement among the Bantu, with one-third of Bantu Christians having come to Christ through Methodism. Internationally, Edwin Orr argues, the greatest extension of the 1858–59 Revival was through William Taylor's work. In addition to England, Australia and Southern Africa, Taylor preached in Asia Minor, Syria, Palestine, Egypt, Ceylon, New Zealand, India, parts of Central America, Brazil, Peru and Chile.

The ministry of Walter and Phoebe Palmer, also Methodists, introduces the topic of the ministry of women in revival, and I will look at this in more detail later in the chapter. Walter Palmer was a successful doctor, and Phoebe had become a leader in devotional meetings in New York in the 1830s. These became known as the 'Tuesday Meetings for the Promotion of Holiness', with Phoebe Palmer stressing sanctification through 'laying all on the altar' in complete consecration.[7] In 1857 the Palmers became involved in a revival in Ontario, especially in Hamilton, but also in other places, including Quebec. The initial impact was in camp meetings among the Ontarian Methodists. On 5 November 1857, New York's *Methodist Christian Advocate and Journal* carried a headline, 'Revival Extraordinary', followed by a report that three hundred to four hundred people were converted over a few days and meetings were attracting up to six thousand people. Reports spoke of this Revival reaching 'all classes', with eminent people such as the mayor of the city 'bowed at the altar of prayer' alongside domestic servants. Hamilton's 'gust of divine power', as it was called, was not led by ministers but by lay people. Phoebe Palmer, as the principal speaker, urged her hearers to 'invite as many as possible' to the meetings.[8]

It is significant that the Palmers became involved in transatlantic ministry after this experience of revival in Canada – their vision was enlarging. By the late 1850s Phoebe's writings on holiness were well known in Europe. In the summer of 1859, the Palmers were in Newcastle-on-Tyne, in north-east England, and on 21 September 1859 *The Times* recorded that Newcastle had become 'the scene of a religious "Awakening" which bids fair to rival anything of the kind which has occurred either in North America or the North of Ireland'.[9] It is important to note, however, in thinking about the rhythms that characterized the Revival, that for the previous year there had been special prayer meetings in Newcastle. Nor was the focus only on the Palmers. Hugh Hanna, the ebullient Presbyterian minister from Belfast, also attracted crowds in Newcastle. The work of the Palmers was part of a larger movement. This was a movement that spread within England, and the Palmers continued to be active in different places over a period of four years, often in Wesleyan Methodist churches but also more widely. In the Midlands, in 1863, for example, they built on the initiatives that had previously been taken by local churches in setting up united prayer meetings, and their ministry affected hundreds of people.[10] Nigel Scotland suggests that fourteen thousand people testified to having been 'justified or sanctified' through their meetings.[11]

All these international evangelists contributed in a variety of ways to the sense of a global rhythm of revival.

Varieties of ministry

One group of evangelists in the Revival in Britain was termed 'gentlemen-evangelists'. These included Brownlow North, Hay Macdowall Grant of Arndilly (in Moray, Scotland) and Reginald Radcliffe. Brownlow North came from a family of Anglican clergy but up to his forties his way of life was notorious for its rejection of Christian values. Then in 1854, at the age of forty-five, he experienced a dramatic change of direction as a result of his conversion. He was never ministerially trained but in his preaching he was particularly gifted in dealing with people who were seeking. His straightforward advice was, 'Go home and read your Bible.' Along with the reading of the Bible, he was committed to prayer, which he described as 'the appointed means of bringing down the Holy Spirit'. North was active in Ireland in 1859 under the auspices of the Presbyterian Church, and the Free Church of Scotland appointed him as a lay evangelist.[12]

Reginald Radcliffe, who was a solicitor in Liverpool, was also an effective evangelist. In Aberdeen, in 1859, the meetings he held in the Music Hall attracted nine thousand people, only one-third of whom were able to get into the building. One convert in Aberdeen, who became a missionary in China, spoke of how the message of Radcliffe was a 'new idea' – 'you only have to believe'.[13] In another fishing town, Lowestoft, in East Anglia, Radcliffe's meetings in the railway depot attracted three thousand people. In East Anglia, Radcliffe received support from Anglican clergy such as J.C. Ryle in Ipswich, who was later the well-known Bishop of Liverpool.[14]

The lay-led Brethren (sometimes called the Plymouth Brethren) movement experienced considerable growth as a result of the Revival of this period, and the work of evangelists was central to this movement.[15] Neil Dickson notes the connection between Radcliffe and home meetings with a Brethren ethos held in Aberdeenshire.[16] R.C. Morgan, the editor of *The Revival*, was associated with the Brethren in Bath from 1851 to 1855, and although he never joined in membership as he felt this would restrict his interdenominational freedom, his association was an indication of his sympathies with lay movements.[17] One notable Brethren evangelist in this period was George Brealey, whose work in the West Country resulted in remarkable conversions in the 1860s and beyond. As an indicator of the anti-clericalism of the Brethren, Brealey's biographer recorded that on a train journey Brealey once met a drunk clergyman who told him that he should not perform the functions of a minister – for example, by baptizing converts – as he had never been ordained. Apparently Brealey's reply was that he had received a higher ordination than had the clergyman, since he had been ordained directly by Christ.[18] Another noted evangelist in this period, Henry Varley, had been a Baptist but had built a Free Tabernacle in 1860. C.H. Spurgeon described him as 'a bad Baptist and a half-bred Plymouth Brother'.[19]

Although there were some typical patterns of evangelistic activity, it was not the case that evangelists concentrated only on some classes of people or on certain rigidly defined types of ministry. William Blair, of the United Presbyterian Church in Dunblane, Scotland, spoke of how he heard Brownlow North address mill workers one afternoon. They were 'in their working habits', he noted, and he emphasized that they 'listened eagerly to the address'.[20] In London, by contrast, North gave three addresses to 'large assemblies of the higher classes, chiefly ladies', and far from dealing gently with his wealthy and sophisticated audiences, North spoke on the parable of the rich man and Lazarus.[21]

In 1858, in Thurso, in the far north of Scotland, Brownlow North and Hay Macdowall Grant had a major impact on a cross-section of people in the town, so much so that the effect was felt in the nearby Orkney Islands. In the 1860s, two young men whom Spurgeon had baptized at the Metropolitan Tabernacle, Rice T. Hopkins and Samuel Blow, became Brethren evangelists. In 1867, they founded a Brethren assembly in Aberdeen and in the same year Hopkins' preaching had a considerable impact in Orkney.[22] Even further north, in the spring of 1860 there were special prayer meetings in the Shetland Islands, and interest in spiritual awakening grew steadily. In 1862, two lay evangelists, Dr Craig and John Fraser, began an evangelistic campaign in the islands and as many as twelve hundred people crowded into the largest church for nightly meetings. The movement of revival carried on for many months.[23]

Hay Macdowall Grant had a major impact in 1859 on the Scottish village of Ferryden, which faces the port of Montrose. Ferryden was a fishing village with a 'rough culture', whereas Grant was a merchant and a laird, but on 9 November his preaching in Ferryden began a revival that lasted for weeks. This was the first Scottish awakening to see physical prostrations similar to those in Ireland. At one of the early meetings, for example, a fisherman was 'seized with a terrible shake', lay on the ground for a time, and felt great gloom and then subsequently thankfulness. The revival led to about two hundred professions of conversion. A local Free Church minister, William Nixon, wrote down the experience of 24 converts who related their stories to him. In a detailed examination of this local revival, David Bebbington has argued that there were cultural movements that came into collision: popular culture; Romantic ideas, with their stress on the human will, promoted by evangelists, such as Grant and Gordon Forlong, who came to the village; and the traditional Calvinism of the Free Church, which Bebbington links with Enlightenment thinking. In Ferryden, the Free Church decisively shaped the revival. Although the visiting evangelists were important, 'the currents of vigorous spirituality in the village ran into the institutions of the Free Church'.[24]

Some evangelists concentrated their whole ministry on a local area. An example is James Turner, a fish curer from Peterhead in the north-east of Scotland. He became a Methodist lay evangelist and his vivid and emotional style of preaching worked well among the fishing communities of the Moray Firth, even though elsewhere it did not. Turner's evangelistic tours of the fishing communities in 1859 and 1860 were the catalyst for the awakening in that area.[25] A reporter for the *Peterhead Sentinel* commented that Turner was 'far from being a cultivated speaker' but considered that the novelty of his language – so different from the 'cut and dry' style of ordinary addresses – and in particular 'the direct, forcible and almost rude appeals to the consciences of his audience, coupled with the deep apparent earnestness of the speaker, produced a manifest impression'.[26] Physical prostrations took place, as in Ireland. Local Presbyterian ministers were anxious to calm the meetings down and when ministers who were opposed to the physical manifestations were present, the phenomena did not occur. However, what was taking place in this local expression of revival was indigenous: conversions took place when Turner was free to preach in his own way and his fellow fisherfolk were free to respond. It was the Methodists who gained most from the revival among the fishing people and new churches were planted in Findochty, Portessie, Portgordon and Buckie.[27]

Another, rather different, example of the way in which an evangelist operated in a manner that produced a response but also provoked opposition is seen in Reginald Radcliffe's ministry. In many places he was well accepted, not least in his home area of Liverpool. At meetings in 1861 in the Concert Hall, Great George Street, Liverpool, he asked a number of those present to leave the Hall and go into the streets, preach, and invite the hearers to the Hall. About a dozen men did so and returned with some people who would never have been found in a Christian meeting. Observers were impressed by the way the people from the streets, with their very evident needs, were received. In the same year, however, Radcliffe preached in Whitefield's Tabernacle in London, and the minister, John Campbell, described his sermon as 'so incoherent that it might have been preached backwards'. These comments by Campbell were reprinted in the Anglican evangelical weekly, *The Record*. John Kent's view is that part of this paper's agenda was to attack the Baptist minister, B.W. Noel, who had sponsored Radcliffe. Noel, as someone who had moved from Anglican to Baptist ministry, was anathema to *The Record*. Kent is right to highlight the tensions that existed, tensions that Edwin Orr fails to note.[28] At the same time, it is not surprising that as these lay evangelists sought to adapt themselves to the situations they found, their activities would prove controversial.

As well as the evangelists whose names became well known because they travelled more widely and were often full-time, there were many others who emerged as local evangelists while continuing in their secular employment. William Gibson, returning in May 1859 to Ulster with J.H. Moore of Connor, after they had attended the meetings of the Free Church Assembly in Scotland, discussed the fact that some young men from Connor were about to visit Belfast in order, as Gibson put it, to 'make known the great things they had witnessed in connexion with the advancement of the work of God'. Gibson, like a number of other Presbyterian leaders, was initially unfavourable to this experiment in lay witness. But Moore, a fellow Presbyterian minister, did not agree. He said: 'I have so often seen how human wisdom has been at fault in this whole movement, that I should not wonder if the employment of such an agency as that in question should be extensively blessed for good, and if the visit of our friends should be only preparatory to a great awakening among your fellow-townsmen.' Moore was right. The witness of the young converts from Connor made a deep impression on the churches they visited in Belfast and within a week 'a feeling of deepest solemnity pervaded the congregations'.[29]

The varied ministries of lay evangelists were, in many cases, in harmony with the rhythms of revival.

In their own language

Another significant group of evangelists was active in Britain in this period – the so-called working-class evangelists. In the 1850s, there was considerable concern in the British context that the Church in general – including many evangelical churches – was out of touch with working-class people, and this was addressed through mission outreach.[30] Local churches that saw the need were engaged in seeking to reach those who were in the growing industrial sector, working in textiles, wood, metal and building, as well as agricultural labourers.[31] Holmes has analysed accounts of 88 evangelists and has found considerable similarities in their experiences. All the working-class evangelists 'gave their childhood and early develop-ments a prominent place in their accounts, many of which reflected the troubled and transitory nature of working-class domestic life throughout the nineteenth century'. For them conversion was a watershed experience, with many able to identify the moment of their conversion.[32] A number had already been engaged in evangelism but they emerged and were utilized in new ways as a result of the Revival.

A typical example of the experience of conversion is the case of Henry (Harry) Moorhouse, who went on to have a signifi-cant ministry as an evangelist. Moorhouse, who before his con-version was always ready for a fight and was also known as a 'prince among card players', was passing by the Alhambra Theatre when he heard a great deal of noise. Thinking that it might be a riot – in which he could become involved – he went inside, to find an ex-boxer, Richard Weaver (who was at one time known as 'Undaunted Dick', after winning a fight that lasted thirty-two rounds), preaching the gospel.[33] That day, Moor-house, together with some of his friends, came to Christ. In his subsequent work he preached in North America as well as in Britain. In 1867, when he was in North America, Moorhouse preached seven sermons one night after another on John 3:16 – 'For God so loved the world.' D.L. Moody, the foremost American evangelist of the time, who had himself felt the powerful impact of the North American Revival of 1857–59, heard this message by Weaver and was deeply impressed, realizing in a new way the importance of the message of the love of God.[34]

Thus, lay evangelists, not least working-class evangelists, influenced others who already were or who became involved in evangelistic work. Often their methods were unorthodox and they did not win the support of all evangelicals, with some evangelical Anglican clergymen being particularly hesitant. William and Catherine Booth, however, who became the founders of the Salvation Army, saw the great potential of these unorthodox communicators. A visit by Walter and Phoebe Palmer to Walsall in early 1863 was followed by an extended visit, for several months, by the Booths. William's open-air meetings drew about five thousand people, of whom three-quarters were men, and Booth realized that a new approach was needed, one that addressed these men – most of them working-class – 'in their own language'. Accordingly, he recruited a team whom he described as 'just of the stamp to grapple with this class, chiefly of their own order, talking to them in their own language, regarding themselves as illustrations of the power of the Gospel'. The original team included Jim Cleaver, known as 'the Birmingham Rough', and William Mee, who had committed the great silk robberies on the Midland Railway. Also on the team was one man who had been so violent that it needed five or six policemen to restrain him. Another had been a horse-racer and professional gambler. Booth noted with approval that they 'were not troubled with any scruples about vulgarity'.[35] It was not that the Booths restricted their attention to those who were obviously distanced from the churches, but that they saw there was a particular calling to the unreached masses.

It was in part out of these experiences that the Hallelujah Bands flourished, meeting a need for what today might be called 'fresh expressions' of church for those who did not fit easily into traditional church structures. It seems that as new approaches were required, lay gifts were used. One of the Hallelujah Bands (known as the 'Flying Artillery', a name taken from North America), which achieved some fame, began to evangelize Nottingham. One report described the members of some of the Bands as including former 'prize-fighters, dog-fighters, prize-runners, gamblers, poachers, infidels, robbers, bear-wrestlers'. Richard Weaver came to Nottingham in 1864 and was followed by another evangelist, G.F. Mather, a former prizefighter who had at that time been converted for only twelve months – through the ministry of the Palmers. The Nottingham Band continued to grow and by 1865 its lay members had taken over a chapel that was dying, with a congregation of only twenty, and held meetings that attracted four thousand people over the course of each week.[36] The Nottingham Band took over all kinds of public buildings, including circus tents, to make the message known.

Often, as was the case in Nottingham in the mid-1860s, one evangelist would start meetings and another would carry them on. Here were rhythms of revival at work. Richard Weaver was followed by Mather, who drew others to the meetings who could identify with his background. Two of the converts were John Homies (also called Jack Rough), a boxer, and Edward Arche, whose career had been in breaking into houses. The dramatic meetings led by Mather were followed by further meetings, led by John Hambledon, who had been an actor before his conversion. Soon this pattern began to be institutionalized. A 'Registry of Evangelists' was developed so that churches could apply for evangelists. Out of this came the Evangelization Society. In some ways this institutionalization was necessary. Wealthy backers were needed for some of the initiatives. For instance, William Carter, a converted chimney sweep, tried to fund Bible carriages in London, but had to abandon his ideas because of lack of money.[37] The organizers

of the Evangelization Society were upper and middle-class
evangelicals, but those who worked for the Society were the
working-class evangelists who were seen to have the necessary gifts to reach beyond the established churches. In time,
however, even controversial figures such as Richard Weaver
became more established. By the mid-1870s, he was a widely
recognized evangelist and also had had a period as a settled
leader of a mission in Hollinwood, Lancashire.[38]

Although working-class evangelistic outreach had a dramatic
effect in the 1860s, by the early 1870s younger evangelical ministers, such as F.B. Meyer, could bemoan the relative failure of evangelical Christianity to draw the working classes in Britain into the
orbit of the churches. In his first ministry, from 1870, Meyer was
assistant to the much-respected Baptist minister, C.M. Birrell, at
Pembroke Chapel, Liverpool. In 1860, Birrell wrote welcoming
the Revival and confessed that he had 'long been oppressed with
the thought of that large part of the population of these counties
which lies beyond the range of religious ordinances'.[39] In Meyer's
next ministry, in York in the early 1870s, he took up that challenge.
Partly through the influence of D.L Moody's ministry in Britain
(which began in York), Meyer and others in this period became
fascinated and excited by new possibilities in evangelism, and
Meyer's aim became to build up a Baptist congregation from
those who had revolted, as he put it, from Christianity as repre-
sented by 'ecclesiastical organisations'.[40]

Yet along with planned evangelistic outreach, there was a continuing desire on the part of Free Church and evangelical Anglican
ministers to experience a fresh revival that would transform society. In 1873, Samuel Garratt, who knew the challenges of work in
urban settings, suggested that 'a mission is no more like a Revival
than a hot-house plant is like a tropical forest', and at a time when
many attempts were being made to reach the working classes he
argued that true revival did not emerge from special plans.[41]

Female preaching

The place of women in revival has been receiving more attention and their role in the Revival of this period was crucial. It

has often been asserted that in the Victorian period the concept of 'separate spheres' was given prominence.[42] The home was seen as the domain of women – especially middle-class women. However, the picture is a complex one. An increasing number of women in Britain were involved in charitable work, with this being seen as an acceptable occupation. For women who engaged in it, such work was a fulfilling way to occupy their time and also an opportunity to move outside the domestic sphere. Many Victorian women who felt a calling from God to Christian service could be found visiting poor areas of cities or towns, selling Bibles, perhaps offering access to nursing care, and giving spiritual counsel. Some raised funds for organizations such as the British and Foreign Bible Society or the Church Missionary Society. Although most of these women were middle-class or aristocratic, working-class women also began to be involved through the pioneering work of Ellen Ranyard who, in 1857, founded the London Bible Domestic and Female Mission. By 1867 this mission employed 234 women, who reached into areas that were far removed from much church life.[43]

Although this kind of work was applauded in the Victorian era, there was limited support within the churches for the idea of women as preachers – unless they were preaching to other women or speaking to children. Most denominations refused to sanction the wider public ministry of women. In Methodism, though there had been women preachers in the eighteenth century, by the mid-nineteenth century there were only a few who were active in ministry. These included Mary Clarissa Buck, a Primitive Methodist. Miss Buck was a popular preacher and travelled vast distances taking special services. At times the crowds wanting to hear her were so large that people had to be turned away.[44] Her work attracted the attention of C.H. Spurgeon. Although Spurgeon did not approve of such female ministry, he did train 'Bible women' as local evangelists.[45] On one occasion he asked Danzy Sheen, a Primitive Methodist who was a student at Spurgeon's College in the 1860s, about Miss Buck. Sheen had recently heard her preaching and gave Spurgeon an account of the sermon. Spurgeon expressed admiration for what he considered an intellectual discourse, describing this as 'masculine', but added that he did not think it was intellectual preaching that won most people to Christ.[46]

The Revival had some specific features that led to the encouragement of women to engage in preaching. Greater involvement of lay evangelists in the ministry of the churches helped church members to affirm that other preachers – including women – could be used by God alongside ordained ministers. Phoebe and Walter Palmer played an influential role in this period. Phoebe never claimed to be a preacher herself, but she wrote defending the ministry of women, defining what they said from the platform as public testimony. Her vision was of lay ministry – in which 'all Christ's disciples, whether male or female', should, as she put it in 1859, 'be endowed with the gift of prophecy', to proclaim 'Christ crucified'.[47] She particularly associated this with the 'last days' before the return of Christ. One of her last publications, *The Tongue of Fire on the Daughters of the Lord*, reiterated this position.[48] Another couple who were prominent in the Revival, Grattan and Fanny Guinness, illustrated that women as well as men had a leadership role. Fanny spoke bluntly of many ministers who were 'useless or worse than useless in the work of soul saving and preach for years without being instrumental in a single conversion', and suggested that there was a case for women's ministry. Janice Holmes comments: 'Biblical restrictions became unimportant; it was simply a case of who was better at saving souls.'[49]

Brian Edwards, who has carried out extensive study of revival, has commented: 'The role of women as preachers during a time of revival is not common, but it is widespread, and instances come from various parts of the world.'[50] Examples given by Brian Edwards are the ministries of William Haslam's wife and of Geraldine Hooper (later Dening), who assisted Haslam – who was a clergyman and evangelist – in his work at Trinity Church, Bath, and later in East Anglia. Hooper, who was the daughter of one of the minor landed gentry of Somerset and was also a friend of Grant of Arndilly, began to preach in 1862.[51] Within Anglicanism, the ministry of women as preachers was highly controversial. When Hooper arrived in East Anglia, a rector's wife in Norfolk, who had been praying for revival for years, wrote to Haslam to say that if this was revival it had come in such a way that she could not thank God for it. Of the visit of Miss Geraldine to the rectory at Buckenham in Norfolk in 1863, Haslam wrote: 'When it was known that she would speak at the barn meeting in the evening, the people came out in crowds, and the place was filled in every corner.' He speaks about her address as 'like kindling a fresh flame'. Local news-papers took up the story. One editor was fiercely opposed, but as Haslam noted, his 'fierce and long articles' did not stamp out the fire of revival but rather 'added fuel to it'. Haslam, who had been converted to evangelical faith in the course of his own ministry, was open to new things – to fresh rhythms.[52]

Olive Anderson has argued that the female preaching that developed in the 1860s in connection with the Revival had a great deal to do with the holiness movement. She notes that the men who responded to this movement had little difficulty in accepting guidance and exhortation from the women who were often its chief exponents.[53] It is overstating the case to say that women were the leading advocates of the holiness move-ment. The movement did, however, give them greater freedom than they would otherwise have had.

David Bebbington shows the centrality of the Mildmay con-ference, founded and led by William Pennefather, to the devel-opment of a British holiness movement in the second half of the nineteenth century. He writes: 'Mildmay introduced a section of the Evangelical party in the Church of England to higher spiri-tual aspirations than were normally entertained in the middle years of the century.'[54] It is significant that an order of dea-conesses emerged from Mildmay. The Deaconess Order, which was initially known as the Association of Women Workers, was led by Elizabeth Baxter, who was encouraged in her ministry by her husband, Michael. William Haslam, who stressed the life of holiness, was a regular speaker at the Mildmay conferences. His associate, Geraldine Hooper Dening, inspired other women. Matilda Bass, for example, was not sympathetic to women preaching but when she heard the stylish Geraldine Hooper Dening speaking in 1867 with 'intense earnestness and enthusi-asm' her views changed and she herself became a preacher.[55]

Among the Brethren, a movement not generally associated with women preachers, there were several women who preached, in Scotland in particular, in the 1860s. Perhaps the best known was Jessie MacFarlane, who had been brought up as a Presbyterian but began to preach in 1862 in Edinburgh as a result of encouragement from a Brethren evangelist, Gordon Forlong, a Scottish lawyer who worked with Radcliffe. Forlong had become convinced about female preaching and wrote a pamphlet in 1863 in defence of the practice. A year later, Jessie MacFarlane herself wrote *Scriptural Warrant for Women to Preach the Gospel*. She extended her own preaching from Scotland to the English Midlands and to London. Another Brethren preacher in this period was Isabella Armstrong from Ireland, who had begun preaching during the Revival in 1859 in County Tyrone. She continued her ministry in Lanarkshire, Scotland, and in 1866 wrote a pamphlet, *Plea for Modern Prophetesses*. Mary Hamilton and Mary Paterson, working-class women from Lanarkshire who were converted during the Revival, also preached in Brethren assemblies in this area of Scotland.[56]

It was on 8 January 1860, during this period of revival, that Catherine Booth announced that she was going to preach. This event took place in the Methodist New Connexion Chapel in Gateshead, when Catherine 'felt the Spirit come' and asked to 'say a word'. Earlier, at the age of twenty-six, she had reached the conclusion that there was a need for the liberation of women.[57] The Booths went on to conduct powerful evangelistic meetings in the 1860s, for instance, in the north-east of England, in Cardiff, in the Midlands and in Cornwall – with seven thousand professing conversion in Cornwall in 1861. The Booths became convinced that there was a strong connection between holiness and revival. From 1861 Catherine stressed the holiness message of 'full consecration'. Tensions between William Booth and the Methodist New Connexion led to his resignation in 1862.

The Salvation Army, founded in 1865 – known first of all as the East London Christian Revival Association or Union, then as the East London Mission, then as the Christian Mission and then as the Salvation Army – was the most significant organization in this period to foster the use of female preaching. Catherine Booth had been inspired by Phoebe Palmer, and in 1861 she wrote the pamphlet *Female Ministry* as a reply to an independent minister, A.A. Rees, in order to defend Palmer's ministry in Tyneside. In this pamphlet she also argued for the ministry of women as appropriate since Christ's coming, and not simply in the 'last times'.[58]

In the early 1860s, part of the Booths' growing operation in the East End of London was a team of twelve women called 'the Christian Female Pioneers' or 'the Female Band'. The leader was Eliza Collingridge, who had been deeply affected at a holiness meeting in Bethnal Green and consecrated her life to Christian service. One of the original group, Caroline Reynolds, spoke of the sensation that the team caused in London. Many people showed curiosity, and some of this, as Reynolds later recalled, constituted a 'great cross' to be borne.[59] The growth of the Christian Mission, as it was then called, multiplied the number of women leaders and preachers. The women came from a variety of backgrounds – Janice Holmes has identified a candle factory worker, a former barmaid, a rag sorter, a domestic servant and a stay-maker. Many of these began work for the Mission when they were in their teens. Some gave up their work after marriage but others continued. A few became particularly well known. 'Happy' Eliza Haynes was famous in Nottingham for driving through the city on top of a carriage while throwing tracts to the people and also – which must have been difficult to do at the same time – playing the fiddle.[60]

This is not to say that the women felt confident in their work or that the congregations always had confidence in them – at least not at first. In Poplar, East London, Annie Davis' impact was overwhelming – initially she frightened the members of a prayer meeting she was running and they all left. However, the dedication of these women became a means of attracting both women and men. Annie Davis built up a successful work in Barking. Her obituary described her as the first of 'a new order of feminine leaders who developed capacity to get together and manage a congregation and society, as well as preach to it'.[61] When William Booth asked Pamela Shepherd –

one of his earliest workers, who had been abandoned by her husband, had lost her job as a rag sorter, and had attempted to commit suicide – to move to Aberdare, she was horrified. Yet her preaching proved attractive.

Sometimes women as well as men were suspicious of women leaders. Rose Clapham, who was a stay-maker, was one of those who showed initial suspicion. To her, the idea of a woman preaching was offensive. She was impressed, however, that the preacher she heard, Annie Davis, wore slippers and not boots and so was judged to be a 'real lady'. She changed her views and she too, at the age of sixteen, became a preacher. Rose Clapham's ministry was one that illustrated the hardships faced by women evangelists. She was refused lodgings and was arrested, yet she also saw remarkable success. In Barnsley, Rose Clapham and Jenney Smith attracted hundreds of colliers to their meetings and built up a congregation of 140 members.[62]

One woman who was to have a significant influence in the 1870s was Hannah Whitall Smith, who in 1858, at the age of twenty-six, had come to a personal experience in which, as she put it, 'my soul was at rest'. Her husband, Robert Pearsall Smith, who was a manager at the Whitall glass manufacturing factory, had a similar experience. Both Hannah and Robert had a Quaker background but were influenced in 1858 by the Brethren. In 1867, Hannah entered a new experience of spiritual victory and she and her husband became leaders of holiness gatherings. Hannah published her bestselling book, *The Christian's Secret of a Happy Life*, in 1875, and in the same year she was the most prominent speaker at a huge event in Brighton when an estimated seven thousand ministers and lay people came together for a week of meetings. Most of those who attended were from Britain but others came from across Europe – from France, Germany, Switzerland, Holland, Belgium, Norway, Sweden, Austria, Italy, Spain – and from India, Russia, Persia, China, Australia, Israel, South Africa and North America. Many of the key speakers were subsequently to become well known for their participation in the Keswick Convention. The Pearsall Smiths would have taken part in the first Keswick, in 1875, but in Brighton Robert made the mistake of putting his arm round a young lady he was counselling and as a result his public ministry was brought to an end.[63] Hannah continued to be influential through her writings.

Conclusion

The Revival of this period has often been referred to as a lay revival. In the previous chapter I tried to show that ministers had a crucial role to play. However, it does seem to be part of the rhythms of revival that lay people are empowered in such times of spiritual vitality and that new movements emerge in which they give pivotal leadership. This phenomenon did not begin in the 1850s but it was a striking feature of what took place in that period. The evangelists were not 'mass produced'. They each had their own personality, used their own gifts, and came from a variety of backgrounds.

The movement that both produced and was given impetus by these evangelists was international. There was also an increased role for women, whose ministry had a powerful effect in the 1860s and beyond. The idea that in revival what the Church normally does is enhanced suggests that, given the rhythms of revival, the intense power cannot be sustained in the longer term, but, at the same time, that the proper release of the gifts of lay people, women and men, is an ongoing responsibility for the churches. This was seen at the time. Samuel Prime wrote:

> Another feature of this work is that it has been conducted by laymen . . . We think we can see a wisdom above measure in so ordaining that this work should commence among laymen – and for the progress of which they should be so extensively enlisted. It has revealed a power which has been dead, or latent, and which even to the present hour is but little understood.[64]

Prime suggested that in all previous revivals a few people had done all the work and 'the hidden, aggregated power of a thoroughly awakened laity was not known'. He argued that in the Revival of the later 1850s the role of lay people had been 'more developed and manifested than ever before'. For him, God had been 'working in such a way as to show more than ever the power of the *Church* – not of the [ordained] ministry only, but of the *Church*'.[65] The ministry of the whole Church is a major lesson to be learned from this Revival.

5

Youth Taking Part

The place of young people and children within the rhythms of revival of the later 1850s and early 1860s was so significant that the topic requires a chapter of its own. This aspect is well illustrated by one feature of the orders of service used in the prominent John Street meetings, as they were usually known, in New York City in that period. An instruction card stated:

> YOUNG MEN AND YOUTH
> ARE AT HOME HERE
> AND MUST NOT
> HESITATE TO TAKE PART!

The stress on 'young men' might suggest that there was no role for young women. It is true that young men, especially those connected with the YMCA (the Young Men's Christian Association), often took the lead. But young women also became involved. In periods of revival within the churches a generation of young people is often affected. It seems that normally the intense experience of revival is not passed to the next generation. On the other hand, it also seems that the impact of revivals is not short-lived. This chapter will suggest that there were longer-term effects after the peak of the Revival. Those whose lives are deeply influenced by revival when they are young often go on to become significant leaders within the Christian community.

Involving young men and women

Many reports in the late 1850s and early 1860s in North America and Britain spoke about the spiritual impact of the Revival on young people. In North America, Kathryn Long writes of a group of younger people affected by the Revival years of 1857–58 – including D.L. Moody, who became the leading transatlantic evangelist of the 1870s and 1880s; the holiness teacher Hannah Whitall Smith; and the mission leader A.T. Pierson. Long describes these and others as a 'revival generation', to be compared for their significance with the 'sixties generation' of the twentieth century. They moved, she argues, like a 'demographic hump' through Protestant North America during the second half of the nineteenth century, promoting through their efforts initiatives in evangelism, in Sunday school work and in overseas mission.[1] A.T. Pierson's son wrote of how his father, who became a formative mission leader, had his convictions about evangelism moulded by the Revival. A.T. Pierson spoke, at the time of the Revival, of how he had begun 'to realize the true worth of souls and the true secret of living near to Christ' and he associated his spiritual experience – a feeling that he had been 'baptized with the Holy Spirit' – with a firm resolution 'never again to pass a day when I cannot feel at its close that I have done something for my Saviour'.[2] Depth of experience and commitment to active service went hand in hand.

The YMCA, which was founded in London in 1844 and was exported to North America in 1851, was indebted to the Revival, especially as this movement among young men developed and grew in North America. The Revival gave it great prominence. The 'Committee on Devotional Meetings' of the New York YMCA, for example, made efforts to contact 'young men who are not connected with the Christian Association, or with any of the churches in the city'. The hope was to find young men who had moved to the city from their home areas and had lost Christian contact. Families at home were used to foster reconnection, with the YMCA playing a crucial role in this process. The 'Committee on Business Men's Prayer-Meetings' in Philadelphia was supported by the

YMCA, which printed and distributed at the doors of the daily prayer meetings, and in other places, tracts containing 'a variety of brief, pointed exhortations, directions to inquirers'. One page was, 'How shall I become a Christian?', which, a report stated, could lead anyone 'directly and simply to Christ'.[3]

Typical of the effect of these efforts in many cities in North America was a young man attending a Presbyterian church in Brooklyn who received a copy of a tract-circular produced by the YMCA, together with a printed card invitation to the John Street prayer meeting. A day or two afterwards, at this meeting, he introduced himself to a member of the Association, and stated that he had experienced conversion through the instrumentality of that tract.[4] In 1863 Moody, then in his mid-twenties, was appointed 'city missionary' for the YMCA in Chicago. Churches had been reluctant to take him on since he was without theological qualifications, but the YMCA offered him the opportunities he needed.[5]

Similar patterns, or rhythms, were to be found in Britain. In 1859, employees at the Woolwich Arsenal in London formed a 'Youths' Christian Association', and hired two rooms for prayer meetings after a visit from a Christian officer, Captain Orr, of the Royal Artillery, who had seen the effects of the Revival in his native Ulster. The Arsenal employed over thirteen hundred young men, and it was reckoned that before the Revival only about six had experienced conversion. The movement in Woolwich spread to nearby Plumstead, where it was reckoned that many previously violent young men were converted. Many of these meetings were addressed by young people. At one open-air meeting the witness of a young man converted in Scotland affected two other young men who had come to listen and also to taunt. The young men were then invited to the chapel of Baptist W. Noel, where Radcliffe was preaching. Other examples were commonly cited by observers in London, for instance, the case of two young men who were 'awakened and converted some months ago, and who are now every Lord's-day evening addressing the people on Paddington Green'. John Weir, ministering in Islington, 'could not help addressing words of caution to them against being puffed up, and so spiritually injured by such prominence', but he was reassured by what he considered their 'unselfish, burning desire to do good'.[6]

The YMCA was influential in London – indeed, London was its heartland. Across the city it was known to have attracted many 'volunteers for Christ'. As a result of the Revival, one branch, in Tichbourne Street, London, had two hundred and fify young men meeting for what was termed 'a Bible reading or devotional meeting' each Sunday afternoon. These YMCA meetings also had an evangelistic dimension. The committed members invited 'associates in business houses', and those who attended were 'not only brought in contact with the written Word, but are specially conversed with, immediately after the breaking up of the class, by persons of their own age, who have been recently led to Christ'. Special speakers were invited, such as Reginald Radcliffe. At the Hanover Square Rooms and the Marlborough Street Rooms, Radcliffe spoke to young men on Sunday evenings. John Weir notes the spirit of prayer 'poured out on young men already Christians'. The same pattern was emphasized: deeper spirituality accompanied by greater commitment to outreach. Weir believed that all across London there was an increasing number of young men marked by wisdom, courage, zeal, devotedness, humility and 'manly piety', and he considered that these young men – many of them connected with the YMCA – would 'speedily stamp their influence on social and commercial life, and prove themselves to be Christ's witnesses and torch-bearers, as well as the attractive exemplars of their generation'.[7]

Although there was a particular focus on young men, reports at the time also spoke of how, at Bible classes conducted by ministers and others, many young women had been converted, especially at the close of the year 1859. Early in 1860 an increasing number of young women began to attend the Friday evening prayer meetings at Tichbourne Street, and on one Friday night in January 1860 special thanksgiving was offered for the conversion of sixteen young women. It was out of these Friday evening meetings that a Young Women's Christian Association (YWCA) emerged. Many of its members were young businesswomen. At Bryanstone Square, as well as Friday meetings, there were afternoon and evening meetings, which included communal meals and Bible reading and prayer. The YWCA also arranged social evenings, and these, too, became powerful spiritual occasions. After one social evening at which addresses were delivered and prayers were offered by Christians present, the YWCA secretary wrote that the subsequent awakening surpassed in interest anything that he had witnessed of a revival character in England.[8]

Many of the meetings in Wales were held in very different settings from those in London, but young people were also central. At one Revival meeting in North Wales, rather than rooms in well-known streets, as in London, the setting was a quarry. In November 1859, the Rector of Festiniog and Maentwrog, D. Edwards, wrote about how revival had come to his Anglican parishes. He reported: 'About three weeks ago a few young men from Bettws-y-coed came to work in the Festiniog slate-quarries. They were in deep concern about the state of their souls. They came on Monday morning, and their deep distress was observed by several of the quarrymen.' After dinner the next day this group of young men went up to the top of a hill to pray. All the workmen in the quarry, numbering about five hundred, followed them. As they prayed, 'the Holy Spirit was poured out upon them most abundantly'. This out-pouring then spread to the local places of worship. 'They met every night during that week at their several places of wor-ship', said Edwards, 'to offer up prayer to Almighty God.' The impact then spread more widely. Edwards noted: 'On the following Saturday those who lived at a distance went to their homes, carrying with them the newly-kindled revival fire, and on the morrow the surrounding churches and chapels were in a blaze!'[9]

On occasions these accounts single out the experiences of individuals. T. Edwards of Penllwyn wrote:

> Not far from this place, a young man, about fifteen years of age, and belonging to an irreligious family, after he was converted introduced domestic worship. His father and brother-in-law were inclined to ridicule; they told him he would require a new prayer each time, and that he must not use the same prayer more than once. By the following Sunday evening the two were

arrested by the power of God's word, to the great joy of the youth.[10]

In March 1859 David Morgan preached at Bethel Baptist Church, Cayo, and reported: 'It was a very hard service.' But the Baptist minister saw things entirely differently, and proved to be right. He wrote: 'It was a remarkable service. The appeals of the preacher were extraordinarily powerful.' Up to eighty people asked for baptism. The subsequent histories of most of them have not been recorded, and it is not possible to be sure about how they all progressed (or otherwise) in their Christian faith, but the first to be baptized, Timothy Richard, became one of the most outstanding missionaries in China of his generation. Brian Stanley describes him as 'an original and controversial missionary thinker without parallel in the [Baptist Missionary] Society's history'.[11] The impact of the spiritual power experienced in revival was felt across the world through those who encountered that power as young people.

Revival among students

Among these young people a significant number were university students. In November 1859, *The Nonconformist* newspaper recorded that a Universities Prayer Union had started, the result of an initiative from Oxford University. It is noteworthy that a newspaper for members of Nonconformist congregations (Free Churches) covered this development, since at that time no Nonconformist was allowed to graduate at the Universities of Oxford and Cambridge. The Prayer Union was to be the beginning of what became a remarkable evangelical movement in these two universities and beyond. Along with the establishment of the Prayer Union, a call was made for special prayer for revival within the universities, a call publicized in the Anglican newspaper, *The Record*, in December 1859. More specifically, Alfred M.W. Christopher (later Canon Christopher) led an appeal for January 1860 to be a week of prayer with a focus on the city of Oxford and its colleges. A weekly prayer meeting was started in the St Aldate's Church rectory in Pembroke Street, Oxford. Christopher was then the Rector at St Aldate's, which came to have a national reputation among evangelicals as a student centre.[12]

Although Alfred Christopher gave important clerical leadership through his emphasis on prayer, much of what happened in Oxford and also in Cambridge in this period was student led. Among the Oxford colleges, Wadham College was regarded as the college most sympathetic to evangelicalism, one of the students, Hay Aitkin, being particularly active in the early 1860s in initiating personal conversations with his fellow students about the Christian faith. Aitkin had experienced the wider revival movement himself in the north of Scotland and had been shaped by it. Reports about what was taking place up to the mid-1860s in Oxford suggest that Hay Aitkin had an influence beyond Wadham College. One report speaks about 'a sort of evangelical revival amongst undergraduates' and refers specifically to Aitkin. A daily prayer meeting also began in Brasenose College, Oxford. Aitkin moved on from Oxford, becoming a widely known and respected evangelist. In 1881, he set up the Church Parochial Missions Society.[13] The effects of the revival in Oxford university continued and a daily prayer meeting was started. Parallel developments were going on in Cambridge. Sunday evening prayer meetings in the university were especially significant, and led to the formation of the Cambridge Inter-Collegiate Christian Union (CICCU), a Union that was to have a significant impact on world mission through students such as the 'Cambridge Seven', who volunteered to go as missionaries to China.[14]

Scottish and Irish universities were affected by the Revival of 1859. In Edinburgh, a medical student was praying with two people who were enquiring about becoming Christians when two prostitutes passed the door and heard what was going on. They returned later and, according to a report in *The Scottish Guardian*, were converted and found new life through a house of refuge, where they lived for two years. The medical student went to a local pawnbroker's shop to redeem some of their belongings and made the dramatic announcement, 'They'll walk the streets no more.' Another prostitute heard this and asked with concern about her friend Bessie: 'Is Bessie dead?'

The student could not resist the opportunity: 'Yes, she's dead and she's alive again.' Out of this event came further ministry to prostitutes in the Canongate in Edinburgh.[15]

In Dublin, one of the students whose life was redirected through the 1859 revival was Robert Anderson, a student at Trinity College. Robert's sister had been converted through evangelistic meetings in the city and she had urged her brother to attend. Although he had not been enthusiastic, he had gone to the meetings, and his life was profoundly changed. Anderson (later Sir Robert) became a leading evangelical layman, well known more widely for his work in directing the CID at Scotland Yard and as Assistant Commissioner of the Metropolitan Police.[16] The impact of the Revival on student life was long term.

In North America, the Universities of Virginia and Michigan were among those affected by the 1858 Revival. At Virginia University a typhoid epidemic broke out among the students and by April 1858 more than twenty had died. One student later wrote about this 'year of sorrow' and of how the students 'thought more about God'. The movement of revival was assisted by the preaching of a leading Baptist, John A. Broadus, pastor of the Charlottesville Baptist Church, who, as a chaplain and a lecturer at the university, had attracted a considerable number of Baptists to become students there. Before the Revival, Broadus had complained about the low level of spiritual expectation in the university, and the fact that it had 'no organized body of believers'.[17] But this all changed. Moreover, the Revival affected not only the university, but also the wider community.

In April 1858 a branch of the YMCA was formed in the University of Virginia and this drew together Episcopal, Baptists and Presbyterian students in almost equal numbers. The YMCA became the agency that directed many of the activities associated with the renewed spiritual life. Prayer and Bible study groups were organized in student rooms near the campus, with an estimated two hundred students (one-third of the student body) participating. Charles A. Briggs, who later became a Presbyterian minister and then Professor at Union Theological Seminary, New York, was typical of the students affected. He joined the YMCA, was converted, and became a member of First Presbyterian Church in Charlottesville.[18]

Two students at the University of Michigan, Adam and Edwin Spence, were central to the movement that took place there. They, with others, were unhappy that the reports on missionary subjects at the university's Society of Missionary Enquiry were given 'in a flippant way and by persons irreligious and even immoral'. They discussed the situation when they went home (to Ann Arbor) during the Christmas holidays of 1857–8 and their mother, Elizabeth Spence, suggested that Adam and Edwin, together with their friends, should form a new group in the University, taking the YMCA as their model. The Students' Christian Association (SCA) was formed and, drawing support from the university President, Henry Philip Tappan – who was a Congregational minister and also a pioneer in the transformation of North American university curricula – prayer meetings and a student visitation plan were organized. One student, George Beck, noted the presence of 'strong revivals of religion' and Methodist, Presbyterian, Congregational and Baptist churches experienced growth. The SCA at Michigan sent a steady stream of graduates into Christian ministry and into other spheres of influence, with Adam Spence joining the faculty and encouraging the establishment of YMCAs on university campuses.[19]

At Harvard and at Yale the Revival also had an impact. At Harvard, which was predominantly Unitarian, the Unitarian chaplain, Frederic Dan Huntington, embraced Trinitarian views after 1858 and initiated well-attended devotional meetings in Appleton Chapel, which was built on the campus in that year. Huntington became an Episcopalian and after his installation as Bishop of central New York in 1869 he pressed for better working conditions. He came to be seen as a forerunner of the social gospel movement.[20]

At Yale University the influence of the Revival was more widespread. A quarter of the student body could be found attending prayer meetings and Bible studies. In 1858, over two hundred students professed conversion and more than a hundred applied to become members of Yale's Congregational College Church. Conant, in his account, suggested that as far as numbers interested were concerned, the revival in Yale was probably without precedent in college settings. It was reckoned that the Revival affected nearly all the students in some way. Conant noted that 'among the converts are some who have been very bitter scoffers, and who were tolerably well armed with the philosophy of the infidel'.[21] On Sundays many students went out in twos to take services in neighbouring towns. One stable-owner allowed his horses to be used free of charge to transport the student evangelists.[22]

Students brought considerable energy to the spread of the Revival.

Children and revival

There is an increasing awareness of the way in which revivals have had an impact on children. Some of the striking examples in the late 1850s are events that took place in schools, which parallel what was happening in universities. Prime writes that at one of the prayer meetings in North America, a visitor from Columbus, Ohio, gave a short report on Christian work in that city. He said that the churches had shared in the general revival and many new members had been added. One of the most remarkable features, however, according to the visitor, was what had taken place in the schools. In the High School in Columbus, all the boys in the school – numbering at least a hundred – had been converted, with only two exceptions. The pupils were from families connected with different denominations, but also from those with no church connection. He reported that no extraordinary means were used. This report was followed by a comment that the schools in Toledo had known a similar experience with large numbers 'hopefully converted'. This particular prayer meeting concentrated on prayer for schools.[23]

There are a number of examples of revival in schools within Ulster, including schools in Ballymena, Coleraine and Armagh. In each case there was a spontaneous revival movement among children. In Ballymena, a schoolboy felt a strong sense of conviction about his sin. His distress was noticed by his teacher, who suggested that another boy in the class should accompany him home. On the way out of the school the two boys started to pray and then felt that they should go back and speak to the class as a whole. The classmates, who might have been expected to ridicule this episode, were impressed and a spontaneous prayer meeting began. Adults in the neighbourhood wondered, not surprisingly, what was going on and came to investigate. The spiritual power in these unexpected prayer meetings conducted by young people in turn affected the adults.

In the girls' school in Armagh it seemed to observers that the Holy Spirit 'was preparing the soil for a special shower of blessing'. One morning a girl came into the school, threw up her arms and exclaimed, 'I have found Jesus!' The effect was described as being like an 'electric sympathy' that 'ran from heart to heart'. The local Presbyterian minister and a visiting Scottish minister came to speak to the children. This movement continued.[24]

In Ireland, more commonly, spontaneous prayer meetings began in churches rather than in schools. In Straid, a mountainous district in the county of Antrim where the people were mainly small farmers and weavers, James Bain, pastor of the Independent Church, spoke of how, in April 1859, news reached them of 'the strange things that were being experienced in other parts of the country'. Bain was interested, but cautious. However, what took place in Straid, including among children in his church, convinced him. On 17 October 1859, Bain wrote to John Ross, a minister in London, about a recent prayer meeting 'held by the children from eight to twelve years of age' on a Sunday before the morning service. As the prayer meeting continued, 'Eight were brought under conviction; such a scene I have never witnessed.' All the children were calling to God for his mercy and Bain's wife and youngest daughter became involved in prayer for the children. Bain's letter continues: 'Leaving the whole [of the meeting] to the children themselves and Mrs Bain, I began the service in the chapel, and when near its close, we heard the song of praise, as they came from my own house, where their meetings are held – entering in a band – all happy in Jesus – taking their seats before the pulpit – twenty in number.' This movement continued in the evening service and in the following week.[25] This is an example of something happening within a children's group in a church but without the leaders of the church taking the initiative.

The place of children in revival was also evident in Wales. A description by W. Edwards of 'very powerful' revival in Breckonshire, in South Wales, highlighted one case in which about a dozen children began to pray and sing together. Two of these, aged twelve and ten, were the children of the owner of a local pub. When they went home they asked their father to join in praising God, and although he said they had 'sung enough' he eventually acceded to their wishes. Children and young people began to hold prayer meetings from house to house. Some people came considerable distances to witness the effects of the revival here.[26] The Rector of Festiniog and Maentwrog in north Wales, D. Edwards, provided another example of the involvement of children in a local community. He wrote:

> I do not believe that there was a worse place than the village of Maentwrog for its size within the principality. It was notorious for drunkenness and revelry, Sabbath- breaking and swearing. You could hear the school children in passing, when playing together, using the foul language learnt of their parents at home, and that often with oaths and curses.[27]

However, all this changed, and in 1860 Edwards wrote about children holding prayer meetings together: 'Where there is a group of houses, they assemble at one of them, and hold meetings, at which they read, sing, and pray together, sometimes for hours.'[28]

Harry Sprange, in his informative book entitled *Kingdom Kids*, offers many insights into the experiences of children in various revivals in Scotland.[29] In the introduction to his book he writes of how reading about the part played in Scottish church history by the prayer meetings of children motivated him to probe further and unearth this story. His view is that the spontaneous occurrence of prayer meetings among children 'may

have been a distinctively Scottish phenomenon'.[30] The phenomenon did occur elsewhere, but undoubtedly the Scottish
examples are very telling. For example, Grant of Arndilly gave
this account of what happened in Aberdeen in February 1859:
'The conversion-work at this time in Aberdeen was largely carried on amongst children from eight to fourteen years of age,
and one day about thirty-five boys asked Mr Rait for the use of
Maryhill School for a prayer meeting.' The evangelists were
concerned about leaving the boys to lead the meeting, and so
an adult was present. But leadership was with the boys themselves. The report continues: 'The boys conducted the meetings
always in a most orderly manner, and read the Bible and
prayed delightfully.'[31]

George Stevenson, a Scottish minister involved in the
Revival in his own locality – Wick, a fishing port in the far
north of Scotland – gave this account of what happened at one
meeting in February 1860. He had spoken in church about
some cases of conversion in past revivals. These stories had
impressed one young girl, who spoke about them to school
friends. Stevenson then became involved. He wrote:

> After I arrived and addressed the school, the concern among
> the children rapidly spread . . . Upwards of a dozen boys held
> a prayer meeting together before going back to school in the
> afternoon. Since then several prayer meetings have been estab-
> lished both among boys and girls. At one time there were about
> a dozen separate children's meetings, some of them very large,
> numbering forty or fifty, who met to pray together.[32]

This impulse to pray was quite spontaneous on the part of the
children. On the last Sunday in March Stevenson preached a
sermon to the children in the evening service. A remarkable
two hundred children were in the congregation and at the end
there was a mixture of prayer, singing and crying. Stevenson
pronounced the final blessing three or four times but each time
those present insisted that the service should continue.

A number of these examples come from 1859–60, but the
movement among children continued into the 1860s. For example, in 1863 a striking movement took place among children in

Findochty, a fishing village in the north-east of Scotland. A number of young men held a prayer meeting among the rocks by the seashore, and as a result they decided to go through the village calling upon everyone to join them in prayer. Several people responded and they all went through the village singing a psalm. Some of the children in the village then decided that they would hold a prayer meeting themselves. They prayed for one another and prayed that those who had not yet experienced spiritual life would come to that experience in a powerful way. The children went to a hall where adults were meeting and it seems that the children began to take a lead. On the following day some of the young men went to an adjacent village and there were further experiences of revival. An eight-year-old boy spoke at one meeting and it was reckoned that his words made such a deep impression that more were converted to Christ at that meeting than on any other occasion in this powerful local revival.[33]

Reaching children and young people

In the period 1857 to 1863 many of the spiritual experiences of children and young people within the areas affected by the Revival began in an unplanned way. Increasingly, however, there was a concern to address the spiritual needs of children and young people through meetings and other events designed specifically for them. This was not new: the Sunday school movement was already flourishing. In North America, Moody was part of this movement. In this period, however, there was greater stress in Sunday school classes on the role of authentic spiritual experience. James Morgan, the minister of Fisherwick Place Church in Belfast, spoke of the way in which revival had affected the Sunday school, where he believed spiritual work was 'more marked and general than in the congregation'. Morgan met with about seventy young people every Sunday evening. He described the way in which these young people, who had shown relatively little interest previously, were now characterized by 'deepest seriousness and attention'. When he was due to preach a special sermon to the children, he found that they were praying for him and for God's blessing on the sermon.[34] The activities taking place in the church had not changed, but the experiences were much more profound.

The need to give attention to children and the possibility of spiritual response from children was defended by referring to past revivals. Weir, in his *Ulster Awakening*, speaks of how Jonathan Edwards recorded in his writings that 'little children were brought to Christ in numbers, in the days of the New England Revivals'. The experiences of the eighteenth century still constituted a powerful precedent and Robert Murray McCheyne was also quoted, since he recorded 'cases of similar early conversions in connection with the Awakening at Dundee, in 1839'. The Revival of the late 1850s was seen as being in this tradition.

In Belfast, in 1859, Berry Street Presbyterian Church held children's meetings at which about three hundred children were present, and it was estimated that 'probably one-third of them had been awakened to a sense of sin, and had found peace in Christ'. The ministers involved in the Revival were in no doubt that 'children need conversion', and that 'when the Spirit comes in power', as was then seen to be the case in Ulster, the children 'share in the blessing'. These meetings attracted children whose parents were not regular churchgoers. At one Berry Street meeting 'two of the boys in very poor attire, one of them barefooted, prayed. They were both but barely able to read their Bibles; they poured out their souls before God, with a fervency that the Spirit of God can alone kindle in the heart'.[35]

Many ministers saw the importance for the churches not only of younger children but also of older children and young people. Francis Wayland, pastor of the First Baptist Church in Providence, Rhode Island, had a concern for individual young people in his congregation. Although during the Revival period he was very busy dealing with adults – Kathryn Long describes him as one of a number of 'frazzled ministers' – he invariably visited the Sunday school, which was held before the beginning of the main service on a Sunday, and spoke to the children for a short time. There was a separate young people's meeting associated with the church and Wayland was often present at that, although he did not interfere in the leadership of the young people's meeting, which was in the hands of his friend, former student, and associate, John L. Lincoln. In 1845, Lincoln had become Professor of Latin at Brown University and although presidencies of colleges were offered him, he was committed to working closely with students. His contribution during the Revival was significant. Wayland left the main teaching of the young people in the church to Lincoln, but would occasionally offer some advice about individuals. 'John,' he would say to Lincoln, 'did you see that boy in the corner? He wanted to speak. He ought to be encouraged.' When Wayland was not at the young people's meetings, he always asked how they had been, and who took part.[36] Revival seems, in this period, to have raised the profile of ministry to young people in church life.

The efforts made by George Müller to care for children and young people had enormous influence. The orphanage work of C.H. Spurgeon, which began in 1867, was modelled to a large extent on Müller's huge orphanage work in Ashley Down. Spurgeon was impressed by the way in which Müller made prayer central to his enterprise. This meant that the orphanage ministry was one that was likely to be touched by revival. Although Müller stressed 'living by faith', and was opposed to publicity about financial needs, his methods of financing his work were in fact more fluid than is sometimes realized.[37] However, spiritual awareness was seen as crucial.

In the history of Müller's orphanage ministry, 1858 was seen as especially notable for the conversions that took place among children and for the 'unprecedented greatness and rapidity of the work which the Spirit of God had wrought'. One of the orphans, Caroline Bailey, who was a Christian, died, and within a few days more than fifty of the hundred and fifty girls in one school began to seek personal salvation. This spread to other parts of the orphanage and about sixty professed faith. In July 1859, in a school of a hundred and twenty girls, more than half were described as being 'under deep spiritual concern' and their experience proved to be long lasting. In January and February 1860, 'another mighty wave of Holy Spirit power swept over the institution'. It began among girls from six to nine years old, then extended to older girls, and then to boys, until over two hundred were enquiring about personal faith. The young people asked to hold prayer meetings among themselves. Out of the seven hundred orphans under Müller's care, about two hundred and sixty were seen as giving evidence of conversion.[38]

This period of revival also saw the emergence of evangelists who directed their ministry mainly to children and young people. The most notable was Edward Payson Hammond, who was born in the Connecticut Valley and in 1858–59 was involved in the Revival in the USA and Canada. In 1860, when he was a student at the Free Church College in Edinburgh, he began to preach at Musselburgh in Scotland, and during this time his thinking about Christian ministry to children was revolutionized. He addressed himself to special meetings for children, which attracted – as one observer noted – 'ragged-looking collier lads, fisher lads' and others who were normally not found in church.[39] Meetings emphasized teaching, singing and prayer. In the following year, Hammond was involved in revival in other parts of Scotland – in Annan, on the Solway Firth and in Glasgow. Wherever he went, there was interest in the conversion of young people. In the late 1860s, Baptist Noel invited Hammond to hold meetings in London, and these led to the founding of the Children's Special Service Mission (CSSM).

C.H. Spurgeon invited Hammond to speak to children at the Metropolitan Tabernacle, and it was reckoned that six thousand children attended. Spurgeon advocated lively young people's meetings, short talks, revival hymns which could be accompanied by clapping, and children's prayer meetings. Every child at the Metropolitan Tabernacle was given a leaflet containing hymns reprinted from Hammond's *Hymns of Salvation*. Many children responded to the invitation to come to enquiry rooms and find out more about coming to Christ.[40] When Hammond returned to London seventeen years after his ministry at the Tabernacle, he found that children who had come to Christ at his meetings were now among the leaders of the congregation.[41]

Conclusion

The place of young people and children in the rhythms of revival deserves careful study. Often those affected by revival as young people have gone on later to take up significant Christian leadership. In the later 1850s, the movement among young people was strategic. The YMCA and the YWCA proved to be vital conduits. Here younger lay leadership flourished. Young people were also to the fore within the movements in the churches. Although the number of university students in North America and Europe was not great in proportion to the total population, they also proved to be an important group, with those affected by the Revival providing significant leadership within the evangelical movement. The important place of youth movements was to become even more evident in the twentieth century, with the emergence of groups such as Youth with a Mission and Operation Mobilisation.[42] Children, as seen especially in the accounts from Scotland (but also from other places), have had their own story of revival, sometimes spontaneously offering a lead that was then taken up by adults.

Consistent with the idea of the rhythms of revival, children's evangelism continued after the first impulse of Revival passed. There were long lasting effects. The Sunday school movement was already valued within the evangelical constituency, but as a result of the Revival of the later 1850s and early 1860s new movements, such as the CSSM, developed. This meant that outreach to children in ways that were relevant to them moved higher up the agenda of many churches. The hopes of early leaders of the Revival that youth would take part were fulfilled in many ways that they could not have envisaged.

6

Church Renewal

One of the many reports from the 1859 Revival in Wales spoke of a local church members' meeting in Trevecca, which developed in an unexpected way. As was usual, two or three people had spoken in the meeting about their spiritual experiences, and they had done so – it was reported – with some feeling and power. The service, in the view of those present, 'was passing off pleasantly, every one feeling that it was good to be there'. So far, however, there was nothing that had not been experienced many times before. There was thankfulness for God's gifts, and also prayer that God 'would give yet more abundant proofs of His presence', but no one expected what then happened. The presence of God was suddenly felt in the meeting. It was what an older generation spoke of as happening when the word was preached in power and the 'outpouring of the Spirit' was known in worship.[1] There are certain features that can be seen in congregations that have been shaped in significant ways by revival. This chapter looks at these experiences of renewal in congregations in the 1857–63 Revival and then considers two specific aspects – singing and the place of the Lord's Supper. Finally, the wider effect of the Revival on denominations is considered. Here is another aspect of the rhythms of revival.

Local church renewal

The impact of the Revival on local church life in many places in North America and Britain was enormous. In New York, the

Thirteenth Street Presbyterian Church welcomed, on one Sunday in 1858, 113 people making their first profession of faith. Of these, 26 were 'heads of families' (women or men were counted), and 53 were scholars in the Bible classes. Another church in New York, the Mariners' Presbyterian Church, was at that time reaching people from 56 different nations. At Eleventh Presbyterian Church, also in the city, several members of the Fire Department and from the police had been converted. At Market Street Church, T.L. Cuyler reported that he soon hoped to welcome 50 new members at the Lord's Supper. At another church in New York , the Baptist Mariners' Church in Cherry Street, a church for seafarers at which Ira Steward was pastor, from 1 January 1858 meetings were held every evening for three months and 101 people were baptized as a result. Many of the converts were seamen, among them men from twenty different nations. The congregation increased from a hundred to five hundred.

Some New York churches were holding days of fasting and prayer. Churches worked together. DeKalb Avenue Church, with J.S. Inskip as pastor, was influenced by the Revival at the height of the financial 'panic'. Over the succeeding year and a half over a hundred and fifty people were converted. A daily united prayer meeting was introduced through DeKalb Avenue Church – meeting alternately in the Presbyterian, Baptist and Methodist churches.[2]

Across the Atlantic, another city where local churches were deeply affected by the Revival was Belfast. Although the Belfast churches operated in a very different context from many of the New York congregations – particularly those in New York with an international outreach – they wished to be open to similar renewal. A good example was Great George's Street, a Presbyterian church in Belfast. Thomas Toye, the minister, who was one of the leaders in the Revival, had founded the congregation at Great George's Street in 1842, beginning his work with meetings in a loft. He was minister there for twenty-seven years. After the Revival began to take effect, the Great George's Street building had to be enlarged.

Toye wrote about how, when 'news of the great awakening in North America reached Ireland', he decided to commence a daily prayer meeting 'for an outpouring of the Spirit in my congregation'. This prayer meeting began in April 1858, and initially attendance was small, but then Toye invited three of the converts from Ahoghill to come and speak, and their meetings proved decisive. In June, conversions began and at the end of the month, when a huge revival meeting was held in the Botanic Gardens, Belfast, Toye considered that 'the glorious work may be said to have commenced with power in the congregation of Great George's Street'. A girl in the congregation gave testimony and then added the words, 'Come to Jesus.' The effect was like an electric shock. Congregations grew until people were meeting in the street and in a garden by the church.[3] The movement in this congregation owed a great deal to news from North America, to prayer, to ministerial leadership, to lay participation and to young people.

In Scotland and Wales, many rural churches were affected by the Revival. An example in Aberdeenshire was the village community of Chapel of Garioch where the Free Church of Scotland minister, George Bain, was very concerned about the 'dead and low spiritual state of the Church'. In 1857, he said he considered that without revival the situation would be 'very poor' in ten years' time. When news of revival in North America and Ireland came to Scotland, Bain made a point of visiting Ireland. His reports contributed to local revival. Bain recalled how in his own church, 'The good news of the revival in North America tended greatly to cheer us.' It was frequently mentioned in services and prayer meetings. News from Ireland stimulated the congregation to the extent that they saw God's 'glorious marching' towards Scotland and, said Bain, 'We set ourselves accordingly to welcome and receive him.' Another prayer meeting was started. It was when Bain was in Ireland, in July 1859, that revival came to his congregation. Bain had invited Reginald Radcliffe to preach in his place, and at the same time had asked friends in Coleraine and Belfast to pray for his congregation. Spiritual awakening was first evident in a group of young girls at a local school. Revival then came to the church, with those converted generally 'obtaining peace in waiting on the Lord Jesus in the course of from one to four weeks'.[4]

In Wales, many congregations of all denominations were affected. A report from Beaumaris on the Isle of Anglesey, North Wales, is typical. A correspondent wrote that there had been 'unmistakable proofs of a Divine influence' and that it was possible to say, 'This is the finger of God.' In late 1858 a movement began in the Independent Chapel. The news of the awakening within the church soon spread throughout the town, 'and all classes attended the services, expecting still further manifestations of the Spirit's power'. It seemed to those who participated that 'a nation had been born in a day'. There were conversions and those who had lost their devotion were restored. 'All the Dissenting churches of the town received large measures of the Divine influence, and upwards of one hundred and eighty persons have been added to their communion.'[5]

One particular case was highlighted in the report from Beaumaris. A young man of twenty-two, who was profoundly deaf, asked for church fellowship and came to the church meeting. In this period, the establishment of schools for the deaf was only just beginning. Very few teachers were available. Most deaf people did not have any access to schooling and they were usually unable to learn to speak or to communicate through sign language – hence the term 'deaf and dumb'. Many deaf people were regarded as hardly rational. The Beaumaris correspondent was at pains to highlight this young man's conversion. Normally a testimony would have been given at the church meeting but it seems that it was not possible for this young man to communicate to the members. His parents, who apparently were already church members, were present. The report highlighted the non-verbal communication that took place: 'No words could pass . . . they could only look at each other, but in that *look* there were volumes of astonishment, sympathy, and love!'[6]

Although the effect on congregations across the main denominations in England is not as evident as in Ireland, Scotland and Wales, there are examples of the power of the Revival. The Baptist congregation in the village of Earl's Colne, in Essex, which was formed in 1786, experienced considerable growth as a result of the Revival. In the 1850s, the church was in decline. Although the chapel could seat 400, in 1859 there were only forty-two members. For some time there was no settled pastor but following the recommendation of C.H. Spurgeon, G.H. Griffith came to preach for two months. The account of the church's experiences states that 'a great spiritual awakening commenced among the Church and congregation, and Mr Griffith received and accepted a unanimous call to the pastorate'. Prayer and powerful preaching went together. Private houses were opened for prayer, and preaching services were held in neighbouring villages. Soon the chapel was much too small and a new chapel, seating 750, was erected. Griffith deposited in the memorial stone a Bible, a catechism and hymn books by Isaac Watts and John Rippon. Earl's Colne was, at that time, the largest Baptist chapel in the county of Essex.[7] Here and elsewhere growth was a direct result of the movement of revival of the period.

A revolution in singing

The fact that hymn books were placed alongside the Bible highlights the way in which, together with preaching and prayer, hymn singing has been at the heart of communal evangelical spirituality. In North America, the many prayer meetings that took place normally included hymn singing. A typical description of a midday prayer meeting noted that 'at twelve, noon, precisely to a minute, the chairman rises and gives out that beautiful hymn, Blow ye the trumpet, blow'.[8] This was a hymn that drew attention to salvation and to the spread of the gospel. Reports spoke of 'soul-stirring hymns' sung by 'animated voices'. People took their own hymn books to meetings; in fact, there was a great demand for hymn books. In North America, the hymn book generally used had a small collection of hymns and could be bought for a few cents. Towards the end of meetings, a final hymn was sung. One hymn often used at the end of the period of prayer in Revival meetings on both sides of the Atlantic was, 'There is a fountain filled with blood', written by William Cowper:

There is a fountain filled with blood
Drawn from Immanuel's veins,
And sinners plunged beneath that flood
Lose all their guilty stains.

It was sung with deep emotion by those who felt that they had experienced the cleansing spoken of in the hymn.[9]

During the first phase of the Revival many existing and well-loved hymns, especially those of Isaac Watts and Charles Wesley, were sung with new devotion – for example, the words, 'My chains fell off, my heart was free'. At a Calvinistic Methodist meeting in Breckonshire, in Wales, held on a week-day evening, the gathering experienced a powerful event in which the young people could not stop singing, and it is significant that new tunes, which were described as 'cold, formal', were not used. Rather, it was old words and melodies, described as 'heavenly', that were employed, and some old people, who had longed for revival, said, 'There it is. That is the very thing that I have longed for.'[10] Among Presbyterians in Ireland and Scotland metrical psalms were used.

In Great St George's Street a psalm which came into its own during the Revival – and was known as the converts' psalm – was Psalm 40:

> *He took me from a fearful pit,*
> *And from the miry clay,*
> *And on a rock he set my feet,*
> *Establishing my way.*
> *He put a new song in my mouth,*
> *Our God to magnify:*
> *Many shall see it, and shall fear,*
> *And on the Lord rely.*
> (*from* The Scottish Psalter)

On one occasion, in the garden beside the church, people continued praying and singing psalms until five o'clock in the morning. Reports suggested that out of the eight hundred people who professed conversion during the revival in Great George's Street Church, forty were converted that night.[11]

Although the older hymns and the psalms were valued, the Revival also brought new hymns to prominence. At a huge meeting at Jayne's Hall, Philadelphia, one of those present, George Duffield, expressed his feelings in a hymn that became one of the hymns of the Revival: 'Stand up, stand up for Jesus'. The theme of prayer is present in this hymn, notably in the words, 'Put on the gospel armour, each piece put on with prayer'. J. Denham Smith, a minister near Dublin, spoke of a range of newer and very personal hymns that had been important in the Revival. The titles included, 'Jesus is mine', 'Joyfully, joyfully onward we go', 'Just now, he will save you', and, 'He breaks the power of cancell'd sin'. Smith argued that a time of spiritual life and growth always included new zeal in singing, citing the experiences of Luther, Calvin, the Wesleys and Whitefield.

Smith gave as an example of the power of hymnody a conversion arising out of the singing of the hymn, 'Now I have found a friend, Jesus is mine'. After this hymn, Smith took the opportunity to ask one of the young people in his congregation if she could say, 'Jesus is mine'. She admitted that this affirmation was not possible. Initially it seemed that she had no hope that this would change. Smith, for his part, prayed that within one hour she would be able to say, 'Jesus is mine'. As she struggled, another hymn was sung – the often-used, 'There is a fountain filled with blood'. The young woman identified herself with the dying thief in the hymn, who found that his sin was forgiven. Finally, Smith observed 'the blackness of despair' giving way to 'peace and joy', and the young lady said: 'Now I can say, "Jesus is mine". I have a hold of my Saviour now.'[12]

The weekly, *The Revival*, recognized the importance of the place of singing not only in certain specific settings – for example, in Wales, the land of song, or among psalm-singing Presbyterians – but in all the areas touched by the Revival. As well as the well-established traditional hymns and newer, shorter songs, among the hymns highlighted as characterizing the Revival were, 'Beneath the cross of Jesus' by Elizabeth Cecilia Clephane; 'Jesus stand among us, in thy risen power' by William Pennefather (written in 1860); and, 'O happy day that fixed my choice' by Philip Doddridge, which was published in *The Revival* in 1861. Elizabeth Codner, who lived in London, in a poem published in 1860 spoke of hearing of 'showers of blessing' that God was 'scattering full and free' and that were 'the thirsty land refreshing'. In essence, her poem was a prayer for this to be the personal experience of those who sang these words. It became a well-loved and widely sung hymn.[13]

It is certainly the case that the real revolution in sung worship came through the 'gospel songs' that issued from the period of the Revival and from the following decade, the 1870s, with the campaigns of Moody and Sankey. In a literal sense, new musical rhythms were heard. But the roots of much of the new music lay in the Revival period. For example, one of the most prolific of the gospel song writers was Philip Bliss of Chicago, who had been deeply stirred by the preaching of Henry Moorhouse in Manchester. Moorhouse, as was often the case in his preaching, was speaking about John 3:16. Bliss subsequently wrote a hymn, 'Whosoever heareth, shout, shout the sound . . . Whosoever will may come'.[14]

Some of the hymns that became popular had little merit as poetry, but they expressed in an immediate way the feeling of the times. One of these was 'What's the news?', which was written by a young Scotsman and was widely sung in North America and Ulster. When it was first introduced in North America, in Philadelphia, a report stated that 'the effect upon the crowded audience was thrilling'.

> *Where'er we meet, you always say, What's the news? What's the news?*
> *Pray, what's the order of the day? What's the news? What's the news?*
> *Oh! I have got good news to tell; my Saviour hath done all things well,*
> *And triumphed over death and hell. That's the news! That's the news!*
> *The Lamb was slain on Calvary. That's the news! That's the news!*
> *To set a world of sinners free. That's the news! That's the news!*
> *'Twas there his precious blood was shed; 'twas there he bowed his sacred head;*
> *But now he's risen from the dead. That's the news! That's the news!*

The hymn continues – over the course of seven verses in all – with many more exclamation marks (six per verse) to celebrate the current Revival, conversions, assurance, and happiness. It finishes on a prayerful and also a triumphant note:

> *And now, if anyone should say, What's the news? What's the news?*
> *Oh, tell them you've begun to pray – That's the news! That's the*
>   *news!*
> *That you have joined the conquering band, and now with joy at God's*
>   *command,*
> *You're marching to the better land – That's the news! That's the*
>   *news!*[15]

A classic description of response to God is found in the hymn 'Just as I am', written in 1835 by Charlotte Elliott and reckoned to be one of the finest hymns in the English language. The sentiments were drawn from the words of a Swiss evangelist and hymn writer, Cesar Malan, who had been instrumental in Elliott's evangelical conversion. These are the first two verses:

> *Just as I am, without one plea,*
> *But that thy blood was shed for me,*
> *And that thou bid'st me come to thee,*
> *O Lamb of God, I come, I come.*
>
> *Just as I am, and waiting not*
> *To rid my soul of one dark blot,*
> *To thee whose blood can cleanse each spot,*
> *O Lamb of God, I come, I come.*

Elliott wrote the hymn when she was – as a Christian – suffering from depression and doubt. She decided to write a hymn that focused not on the contribution of human effort to spirituality, but on divine acceptance through the cross. This hymn became very popular through its introduction to a wider public during the 1859 Revival and it began to be used as part of evangelistic appeals. What is less well known is that at the noon prayer meeting in Ninth Street Reformed Dutch Church in New York, this hymn was turned into an evangelistic hymn entitled 'Just as thou art', which became an exhortation from Christ:

Thy sins I bore on Calvary's tree;
The stripes thy due were laid on me,
That peace and pardon might be free –
O, wretched sinner come.

Each of the verses carried the invitation to different needs or perhaps to one person with a variety of needs – to guilty, wretched, weary, needy and trembling sinners.[16] This was clearly a 'gospel' hymn, a hymn of revival.

The Lord's Supper in worship

Another aspect of worship that has been important in times of revival has been the celebration of the Lord's Supper,[17] and this illustrates what is constant in worship, yet is also heightened at certain times. At the local church gathering in Trevecca, Wales, in 1859 (see p. 88), the 'sacrament of the Lord's Supper' was celebrated and it was recorded that 'an influence was felt by all present, which we had never experienced in the like manner before'. The minister spoke to the people and there was 'a beauty, a loveliness about the Holy Word which we had never hitherto perceived'. After a time of deep emotion, those present took the bread and wine but in the singing of the last hymn they found that it seemed impossible to bring the meeting to an end. The last two lines of this hymn were sung for a quarter of an hour. The minister prayed:

> [A]nd such a prayer we had never before heard uttered. We felt that we were communing with God. Our hearts were truly poured out in praises and supplications. We could have prayed all night. But at length the prayer terminated, and we were to separate. But did we separate? Ah, no, every one resumed his seat and kept silence, and there we were for a length of time under the most heavenly feelings.[18]

The meeting continued for four hours. It was described by those present as a kind of Pentecost.

William Arthur, who visited Ulster during the Revival, noted the importance of Communion for spiritual revival. Among the Presbyterian churches at that time the Lord's Supper was administered twice a year and these Communions were occasions of great solemnity. In Ballymena, the 'Spring Communion' in 1858 came at a time (Arthur noted) when the parish had been more or less filled with news of the prayers for revival that were being offered, 'and of the strange, clear, happy conversions which had taken place' – conversions that made those who had been changed go on their way 'walking, and leaping, and praising God'. As the congregation preparing for Communion heard more about the Revival in North America and about the need for revival, it was clear that a deeper spiritual work was taking place – during, as Arthur emphasized, the 'solemn services of the Communion'. Many spiritual experiences were expressed during this period, including 'strong crying and tears, nights spent in wrestling prayer, hearts heavy, and faces mournful with the burden of sin'. Others in the parish were busy 'telling as simply as babes, and as happily as primitive Christians, of God's pardoning love'. As a Methodist, Arthur was impressed that these 'staid Presbyterian folk' were entering into these varied and often emotional experiences, but in reality this was consistent with the range of experiences known at Communion.[19]

In Scotland, as had been the case among Presbyterian congregations in Scotland during the eighteenth-century Revival in 1859 and on into the 1860s, the special seasons of Communion were significant. For example, the Free Church of Scotland minister in Banchory Ternan, who saw a number of people 'awakened and changed', and then become the means of 'awakening others', spoke of the way in which the Spring Communion in May was felt by many to be 'a very solemn season to their souls'. Reid planned additional Communion seasons – anything from two-day to five-day events, sometimes with open-air preaching – since, as he stated, he believed in their power to 'have a beneficial effect and serve to advance the Lord's work in our midst'. Another Free Church minister in the same region, George Bain, had a similar experience, with his church records noting 'a truly wonderful awakening', which took place at a special Communion. More communicants joined the church than in the previous nine years. At one Communion – which was arranged 'specially in connection with the blessed work' (or revival) – fifty new communicants were added.[20] Clearly this dynamic was not the same as that experienced by churches that celebrated Communion more frequently, but the heightened sense of God's presence at the Communion season does seem to have led in some cases to a desire for more frequent celebration of the Lord's Supper.

The movement in this period that did place great emphasis on frequent – weekly – observance of the Lord's Supper was the Brethren movement. The terminology used by the Brethren for Communion was the Breaking of Bread. Although there were worries among leaders of the Revival about the Exclusive Brethren, led by J.N. Darby, the Open Brethren were, on the whole, well accepted in Revival circles. The new converts were often open to new ideas and one of the ideas promoted by the Brethren was that in the early Church believers met each week to 'break bread'. At the Breaking of Bread meetings there was openness to ministry from gifted brethren, and often a spiritually intense atmosphere, which was attractive to those who felt constricted by ministerial leadership and were seeking deeper spirituality. The common Brethren view was that they reached their conclusions about such matters as the Breaking of Bread through study of the New Testament. However, there were clearly features at work in this period of Revival that assisted their growth. For example, William McLean, a Baptist in Peterhead in the north-east of Scotland, left his church as a result of a local awakening – possibly the preacher was Jessie MacFarlane, who began her ministry in 1862 – and established a Brethren assembly. Such converts to the Brethren influenced others. David Rae, an Irish evangelist, spoke of how he had embraced the practice of weekly Breaking of Bread by reading the New Testament, but in fact he had learned this from McLean.[21] Brethren ideas of worship flourished in the atmosphere of Revival.

C.H. Spurgeon, although an admirer of Brethren figures such as George Müller, could also be a sharp critic of the

Brethren. He questioned aspects of their approach to Bible study, suggesting in 1869 that their priorities in biblical inter-pretation were misguided. 'Plymouth Brethren', he told his students, 'delight to fish up some hitherto undiscovered tad-pole of interpretation and cry it around town as a rare dainty. Let us be content with more ordinary and more wholesome fishery.'[22] However, Spurgeon did share with the Brethren a commitment to weekly Communion. Preaching at the Metropolitan Tabernacle in 1861, in an atmosphere shaped by revival, Spurgeon described past Communion services in 'the darkness of the catacombs of Rome, where only a tiny taper afforded light', and in the present time in 'the far-off isles of the sea'. I may say, he declared in dramatic style, 'O sacred Eucharist, thou hast the dew of thy youth'.[23] The use of the term Eucharist suggests a 'high' view of the Lord's Supper. Spurgeon affirmed his belief 'in the real presence, but not in the corporeal presence' of Christ in the Supper. 'We believe', he said, 'that Jesus Christ spiritually comes to us and refreshes us, and in that sense we eat his flesh and drink his blood.'[24] At the heart of Spurgeon's theology of the Lord's Supper was the con-viction that Christ was present among his people as they took bread and wine. This conviction was expressed in the Com-munion hymn that Spurgeon wrote in 1866:

> *Amidst us our beloved stands*
> *And bids us view his pierced hands.*
> *Points to his wounded feet and side,*
> *Blest emblems of the Crucified.*

For Spurgeon, this awareness of the presence of the crucified and risen Jesus was associated with the gathering together of a group of believers, whether large or small. In a sermon deliv-ered in 1866, 'The Lord's Supper, Simple but Sublime!', Spur-geon spoke about the impossibility of celebrating alone. 'I must have you with me,' he said, 'I cannot do without you.' He referred to groups he had met with as he travelled, and with whom he had celebrated the Lord's Supper in hotel rooms in different parts of Europe.[25] A communal spirituality – which characterized revival – was affirmed.

It has often been thought that the trend towards frequent Communion in the Church of England in the nineteenth century was attributable to High Church influences. But significant Anglican evangelical leaders were in favour of frequent Communion.[26] At a time when many Anglican churches had a quarterly Communion service, a number of Anglican evangelical leaders who were committed to reaching the working classes advocated at least a monthly celebration of Holy Communion and also introduced evening Communions since many people in domestic service worked during the day on Sundays.[27] The need to minister to them was accentuated as a result of the 1859 Revival. The Earl of Shaftesbury was one who called for Anglican ministers to administer Communion on Sunday evenings so that the poor could attend. He was highly critical of the conservatism of some Anglican clergy, as is evidenced, for example, by his statement:

> Now if it were given out by a large body of the ministers of the Church that they would administer the Communion in the evening, many of the poor with whom we have to deal would be likely to attend; but if it is to be given out that the ministers of the Church of England will never consider their convenience and necessities, they will certainly stay away from the churches altogether.'[28]

The rhythms of revival included the rhythm of more frequent Communion.

Denominational effects

The major denominations in North America and Britain all experienced renewal, although to varying degrees, as a result of the Revival. In North America, the Methodist churches gained most new members, about two hundred thousand, with over a hundred and thirty-five thousand joining the Methodist Episcopal Church – which was North America's largest and most evangelistic denominational body at the time. The number of new members added to Methodism in its various forms in Britain – Wesleyan, Primitive, New Connexion, Free Churches and Bible Christians – was approximately the same. In Ireland, the Methodist Conference of 1860 stated, regarding the Revival, that 'all our ministers and people entered into it with holy enthusiasm'. The Methodist New Connexion Conference of the same year spoke of the remarkable power of the Holy Spirit in some circuits as comparable to anything ever known, a striking claim given the history of revival within Methodism. However, the Wesleyan, New Connexion and Primitive Methodist Conferences of 1861–2 all pronounced against the use of non-Methodist evangelists. There was a concern to 'promote Revivals of religion' but also to 'prevent irregularities'.[29] In worldwide terms, Methodists probably gained most from the Revival of this period. Methodist growth in Australia, for example, was massive – the increase was 300 per cent in 15 years.[30] It seems clear – as indicated earlier (see p. 52) – that the greatest extension of the Revival by any one individual was by William Taylor, a Methodist who, like John Wesley, saw the world as his parish.

In the Episcopal Church in North America, the 1858–59 Revival had an impact that to some was surprising. New York had a strong Episcopal presence and the New York Diocese reported a 20 per cent increase in communicants between 1856 and 1857, and 1858 to 1859. In some places, the number of confirmations more than doubled, with numbers in one parish growing from 170 to 500. Benjamin Cutler, of St Anne's Church, Brooklyn, said that twenty years earlier, revival meetings in the Episcopal Church would have been denounced as 'Methodistical': he was delighted that the Church was now 'making full headway in the river that flows from the city of God'.[31] Across the Church of England and the other Episcopal communions – Scotland, Ireland and Wales – opinion within the leadership was divided. John Kent points out that the Church of England had no tradition of recurrent 'revivals' and that the failure of Anglicanism to embrace the Revival was a reason for what he deems the Revival's failure.[32] On the other hand, the claim was made by Edwin Orr that a quarter of a million converts were gathered into church life by the evangelicals in the Church of England. The Bishop of Hereford,

R.D. Hampden, was one of those who attacked what was happening in Ireland in 1858 as 'savouring of John Wesley'. For him, this was a reason to oppose it, but for other Anglicans it was a commendation.[33] Eugene Stock of the Church Missionary Society, who was fully behind the Revival, suggested that if Anglican clergy had more fully embraced the Revival, its effects in the life of the Church would have been greater.[34]

Presbyterians in North America were divided into 'Old School' and 'New School' – a division resulting in part from attitudes to revival – and it is significant that among the 'Old School', reports in 1858 indicated that 70 out of 117 presbyteries had experienced particular blessing, with powerful prayer meetings, new dedication, work among youth and conversions. In 1859, eleven new presbyteries were established.[35] The fact that the Revival prayer meetings started in a Dutch Reformed setting, in Fulton Street, New York, was important for Presbyterians. In Ulster, one-third of the population was Presbyterian, and the impact among this community was massive. William Gibson notes that at the first Communions of the Revival period over ten thousand new communicants were added, and many others who had lapsed were restored. He then adds twenty-five pages of detailed reports from local congregations.[36] In Scotland, adherents of the three main branches of Presbyterianism – the Church of Scotland, the Free Church and the United Presbyterians – comprised over two-thirds of the population of three million. The main stream of the Revival was within the established Churches, although there were itinerant lay preachers whose sympathies were interdenominational, and the number of converts in Scotland is estimated at three hundred thousand, the great majority adhering to Presbyterian congregations.[37]

Baptists in North America were, in almost all cases, fully supportive of the Revival and gained many converts. It has been estimated that in 1858 the various Baptist bodies baptized a hundred and fifty thousand new believers. Among the noted Baptist evangelists in this period were Jacob Knapp, who conducted extended evangelistic meetings in Boston in 1860 and also preached vigorously against slavery, and A.B. Earle, whose work crossed over denominational boundaries.[38] In

England, as a result of the Revival, Baptists probably gained more new members than any other denomination. Of the quarter of a million church members in Baptist churches in England and Wales in 1865, a hundred thousand had come to faith in Christ as a result of the Revival. In 1868, the Home Mission Society reported that 'not a single church had been without additions'. There was great stress on the role of the local church but there was also wider involvement in the Revival by Baptists, with Baptist Noel acting as one of the main spokesmen of the Revival and William Brock, the minister of Bloomsbury Chapel, speaking, in 1859, at London's first theatre service.[39]

It is also possible that the spirit of cooperation evident in the Revival affected Baptist denominational identity. While Baptists were very ready to associate with other evangelicals, they sometimes struggled to work together as Baptists. Many churches felt isolated from the wider denomination and were not even members of the Baptist Union. However, in 1868, the *Baptist Magazine* noted a change: 'The isolation which has so long characterized our body is yielding fast to a general growth of Christian love.'[40] There were several reasons for this, no doubt, but since the Revival was so significant for Baptists it is probable that it had its effect in this 'growth of Christian love'.

In Wales the bulk of the population adhered to the various branches of Evangelical Dissent. The Calvinistic Methodist Church, the Congregationalists, the Baptists and the Wesleyan Methodists gained, between them, about ninety thousand new members during the Revival. Historically the first three of these denominations in Wales, by and large, had been associated with traditional Calvinist views, while the Wesleyan Methodists were Arminian in their convictions.[41] But despite differences, all became involved in the Revival. The 1859 Assembly of the Congregational Union of England and Wales met at Aberdare during the Revival and as well as affirming the Revival in general terms, drew particular inspiration from what was happening in Wales and in Ulster. Their report spoke about an open-air meeting near their Assembly that attracted fifteen thousand people. Within two years the Congregationalists in the county of Carnarvon alone had built twenty new chapels because of the influx of new people.

In England John Angel James, at Carr's Lane, an influential Congregational church in Birmingham, was one of the leading advocates of the Revival within Congregationalism. In 1860, Congregational reports spoke of 'a remarkable revival of religion in the north of Ireland' and of Wales being 'visited to an extraordinary degree'.[42]

Although the Methodists, Congregationalists, Baptists, Presbyterians and Episcopalians were probably the mainstream denominations with the largest numerical growth as a result of the Revival, other churches were affected. In North America, a Lutheran weekly newspaper observed in March 1858: 'The religious interest in our [Lutheran] churches as well as in other denominations is so general and widespread that ... it is impossible to chronicle in full all the accounts.' The Old Mennonites – the Mennonites, as a denomination, had their roots in the sixteenth century and in the leadership of the Dutch Anabaptist, Menno Simons – were deeply affected by the 1858 awakening in Pennsylvania and the Midwest. John Fretz Funk, who was converted in 1858 in Chicago under Presbyterian influence, and was baptized a year later, became a major leader in the Mennonites. He helped them to organize Sunday schools, mission boards and publications, notably the *Herald of Truth*, the first Mennonite periodical in the United States. A new denomination was also launched, the General Conference Mennonite Church.[43] The Quakers in Britain – and in North America – also gained new members after a period of decline. One movement that grew rapidly, as has already been seen, was the Brethren movement. The Brethren tried to avoid statistics of membership and did not see themselves as a denomination. A survey of Brethren biographies, however, gave Edwin Orr the impression that the Brethren may have gained more from the Revival than any other body.

Most denominations gained greatly from this period of Revival, but the more powerful influence was transdenominational. This was recognized on the first anniversary of the beginning of the Fulton Street prayer meeting. The most striking feature of this anniversary meeting was judged to be 'the cordial and affectionate union of ministers and private Christians of so many different denominations in celebrating the sacred occasion'. Thomas de Witt, Senior Minister of the Collegiate Dutch Churches, presided. In the first part of the service Baptist and Presbyterian ministers took part. Speakers referred to the changes that had taken place in the spiritual atmosphere in the business quarter of New York over the previous twelve months. The venerable Nathan Bangs, a distinguished leader in the Methodist Episcopal Church, asserted that this was 'the first successful attempt at Christian union which had been made'. This statement did not take into account the formation of the Evangelical Alliance in 1846, no doubt because this was not a success from a North American point of view. Bangs confessed that for a great part of his ministerial life he had 'battled with other denominations', but of late he had been preaching on 'Love'. At the end of the meeting Theodore Cuyler, from Brooklyn, led in prayer.[44] Denominational distinctives were secondary to spiritual unity.

Conclusion

In this chapter I have tried to explore some of the dynamics at work in the congregations and the wider church groups – the main denominations – that felt the impact of the Revival. What seems to have characterized those communities that were reconfigured by revival was, first, a greater openness to the immediate presence of God in worship and, second, in the area of outreach to those in the wider community, a new stimulus to creative action. In many places, the churches attracted new converts without engaging in organized mission activities, although there was often a strong link between the place of prayer in revival and an outward-directed spirituality. As has been noted in Chapter 3, preaching was crucial.

This chapter has looked at the singing that characterized revival meetings, with both older hymns and new songs being sung. The congregations and the associated meetings of an inter-church nature were keen to express in singing all that God had done. There was an openness to what God would do and a heightened sense of the presence of God in the celebration of the Lord's Supper as well as more widely in all parts of worship. I have not wanted to focus on the emotional side of what takes place in worship. That is not unimportant, and is certainly not something to be dismissed, but the major stress is on the way in which the different elements of congregational life become energized in new ways. It is not that churches and groups that experienced revival found that heightened experience became the norm – indeed, the theme I am pursuing of rhythms of revival would suggest that the idea of reaching a point from which there is continuous revival is not the way to approach the subject. But there was a period when significant experience of God was known, and this had long-term effects.

7

The Gospel in Society

The growth of the church accompanies and in part defines revival. The definition by R.E. Davies is worth repeating:

> A revival is a sovereign outpouring of the Holy Spirit upon a group of Christians resulting in their spiritual revival and quickening, and issuing in the awakening of spiritual concern in outsiders or formal church members; an immediate, or, at other times, a more long term, effect will be efforts to extend the influence of the Kingdom of God both intensively in the society in which the Church is placed, and extensively in the spread of the gospel to more remote parts of the world.'

Davies speaks about an immediate or more long-term effect being outreach. The idea of rhythms of revival is helpful here. The initial movement does bring people to Christ, but that is not necessarily the focus, and the way in which that happens initially is often not through organized means. However, other effects follow. Such outreach, in the period being examined here, was often a fruit of prayer for revival. Some aspects of mission have already been covered in looking at ministers, at lay evangelists and at young people, but this chapter explores in more detail revival-related outreach, effects within society and the wider missionary impetus.

Initiatives in cities

In the period of the Revival, both cities and rural areas were affected. As planned outreach supplemented spontaneous awakening, there was a particular concentration on cities. Baptists in London expanded greatly, with numerous new congregations being planted. Outreach that began in Wandsworth, south London, in 1859, for instance, brought into being East Hill Baptist Church. Under John W. Genders, the young pastor, meetings were started in the Assembly Rooms of the Spread Eagle Tavern; by the mid-1860s the membership was over a hundred and fifty, with many more attending. A chapel was erected costing £3,000.[1] An inn was also used as a venue in Bromley, Kent, where meetings were started in 1862 in the Assembly Rooms of the White Hart. Archibald G. Brown, aged nineteen and still a student at Spurgeon's College, saw the Bromley congregations grow from about thirty to two hundred in a year. In 1863, a church was formed with twenty members and two years later it was reported that a large chapel was being erected.[2] The East London Tabernacle, Stepney Green, which became the second largest Baptist church in London, met initially in the Beaumont Hall, Mile End Road. Student preachers drew up to two hundred people to the East London Tabernacle in the early 1860s, and a chapel seating eight hundred was erected in 1864. Archibald Brown moved from Bromley to East London and under his ministry Sunday evening congregations (which in churches of this period were always larger than Sunday morning congregations) soon grew to twelve hundred people, with a membership in 1868 numbering five hundred.[3]

Periods of revival have often produced new forms of outreach, and events in London offer a good example. As well as involvement in church planting, other ways were found through which – as Edwin Orr puts it – 'awakened Christians in London soon found an opportunity of harnessing the flowing tides of Revival'. One new initiative in the 1860s that Orr discusses was the use of theatres for evangelistic meetings. The Earl of Shaftesbury, the most prominent evangelical social reformer in the nineteenth century, was at the forefront of this new development. In 1855, Shaftesbury had sponsored a Religious Worship Act to allow services involving Anglicans to take place in 'unconsecrated' buildings. There was opposition from High Church Anglicans, but an ecclesiastical compromise was reached, and on New Year's Day 1860 the Britannia, Garrick and Sadler's Wells theatres were used for the first time as venues for Sunday evening services, attracting huge audiences. By February 1860 seven theatres in London were serving as preaching centres, with both Anglican clergymen and Nonconformist ministers preaching. A total of twenty thousand people attended these new forms of services.[4]

This adventurous approach to outreach required a new type of preaching. Shaftesbury, while opposing some new ventures, such as the Salvation Army, was enthusiastic about the young preachers who were associated with C.H. Spurgeon (some of them students) whom he heard speaking at services in theatres. He noted their colloquial way of addressing people who would not find ordinary services comprehensible. Shaftesbury, although himself a committed Anglican, had no faith in High Church ritual – he spoke dismissively of 'bits of wax candle' and 'gymnastics in the church' – but he applauded the evangelistic work of 'the pupils trained in Mr. Spurgeon's College'.[5] A move was made in the House of Lords to stop the theatre services but Lord Shaftesbury made an effective speech about the need to reach those outside the churches. He referred to an observation made by an Anglican clergyman in Lambeth, who had been a missionary in Sierra Leone. The former missionary believed that the spiritual and moral conditions in Lambeth were worse than in Sierra Leone, and this bleak assessment was a good reason, in Shaftesbury's view, for seeking to reach those who had no contact with the Church.[6]

As well as ministers and theological students who adopted their style for speaking in theatres, some of the lay evangelists found these kinds of venues congenial, including working-class evangelists, as already noted in Chapter 4. Richard Weaver began services in the Victoria Theatre, Waterloo. There was a high degree of entertainment in the conduct of these services, with Weaver's style fitting perfectly into this atmosphere. He once announced: 'There's a thief somewhere here tonight, that's come to pick pockets. I can't point thee out but God knows thee; there thou art, and thy name is Thief.' Weaver announced that the thief had been in prison and would be in an eternal cell unless he repented.[7]

After four years of services in Waterloo, it was estimated that over eight hundred thousand people had attended, although probably not many of these were regulars. Sunday afternoon meetings were arranged for those who wanted to enquire further about the Christian faith. The founder of what was London's chain of 'J.P.' restaurants was brought to Christian commitment through meetings led by William Carter. Reginald Radcliffe, another of the prominent lay evangelists involved, called a conference in January 1861 to talk about the needs of the East End of London. Baptist Noel, who was present, promised that out of the East End would come future 'Luthers and Whitefields' to spread the gospel. As a result of this meeting, an East End Special Services Committee was formed, which took responsibility for services in the Garrick Theatre in Whitechapel. The Salvation Army can be seen as a fulfilment of Noel's prophecy.[8]

Although quite a number of the new initiatives in Britain in the 1860s were to be found in London, the adoption of new ideas in other cities was significant. In Birkenhead, in the north-west of England, for example, the YMCA was able to utilize the Theatre Royal for preaching. Beginning in December 1860 there were weekly Sunday evening meetings, which attracted large numbers. Among those converted in Birkenhead in this period was Samuel Smith, later an MP and Privy Councillor to the Queen.[9] A year after the Birkenhead Theatre meetings began, Reginald Radcliffe started his Sunday evening meetings in the Concert Hall in Liverpool and this became a centre where a whole succession of lay evangelists spoke. By 1864 the Free Trade Hall in Manchester was being used for similar meetings, with one of the speakers being Arthur Stevenson Blackwood, who was later the senior executive of the Post Office (then Britain's largest employer) and was knighted for his public service. Theatres and other large buildings were utilized – and filled – in cities such as Sheffield and Leeds. A newspaper report in 1863 said that four meetings in the Amphitheatre in Leeds, at which Richard Weaver was the speaker, had attracted a total of twenty-two thousand people and declared that there had seldom been such excitement about religious service in the city.

In the early period of the Revival there was an emphasis on prayer and on renewal, while by the early 1860s much more attention was being given to new methods of outreach, the old methods being deemed to be inadequate.

Social consequences

Continuing debate has characterized the attempts to quantify the changes in society brought about by the Revival. Kathryn Long has argued that a concentration on personal piety in the wake of the Revival meant that larger, pressing social issues in North America, notably slavery, were not addressed. George B. Cheever, minister of the Congregational Church of the Puritans in New York, welcomed the Revival as a 'season of refreshing from the presence of the Lord', but – controversially – he argued that the Revival was distracting evangelicals from the issue of slavery. Among those affected by the Revival, ethical concerns were being addressed, but they were often about vices such as drink and gambling. Cheever believed that the Bible needed to be applied not only to personal sin but also to the 'political sin' of slavery.[10] Long argues that in the period of the Revival what emerged was 'a more socially conservative view' in which evangelicals stressed the importance of evangelism, believing that changed individuals would produce a changed society.[11] However, social conservatism was evident among evangelicals in America in the years before the Revival began. For instance, a decade before the Revival, when attempts had been made to form a World Evangelical Alliance, North American evangelicals had rejected a British proposal that slave-holders should not be allowed to be members of the Alliance.

It is certainly true that writers such as Samuel Prime stressed the power of individual conversion. He wrote that New York was incredulous when it was announced that Orville Gardner, or – as he was usually nicknamed – 'Awful Gardner', had come to a union prayer meeting. He was a notorious boxer who on one occasion bit off another boxer's ear in a hotel brawl and in 1855 had spent time in prison for starting a fight and breaking a businessman's jaw. Prime reported that Gardner had entered new life and was an active Christian. Indeed, Prime had concluded from information he had received that several thousand people had given up lives of crime. Prime also commented that there had been a fear in New York that the financial crisis, which had caused mass unemployment, would mean that 'life and property here were not safe' if 'unemployed masses tramped the streets with banners, demanding bread'. But he was glad to report that Christian action had been effective: by personal visitation, by extraordinary efforts to relieve the distresses of the needy, and by Christian sympathy, people's hearts had been changed.[12]

However, one aspect of the story of the Fulton Street prayer meeting reveals a retreat from those needy people. When Jeremiah Lanphier was first employed by the North Dutch Church, it was primarily to reach the poor around the church – often immigrant families. In the event, his ministry became directed to the business community. Other groups, also, found the atmosphere of some of the meetings uncongenial. In March 1858, an African American wrote to the *New York Daily Tribune* to say that when he and a woman, also an African American, had arrived at the Fulton Street prayer meeting, they had been shown to an empty room on another floor and told that 'the colored people have good meetings "up" here.' They left, hoping to find 'the blessings of the outpouring of the spirit elsewhere'. Women, too, who wanted to contribute to these meetings found that this was not welcome. Maggie Van Cott, who was involved in managing her invalid husband's business, attended the Fulton Street meeting once and spoke briefly about 'the power of Christ to save'. On the way out she was told that this was not a meeting where women could speak. Mrs Van Cott later became the first women licensed to preach in the Methodist Episcopal Church in the United States. Prime was glad that Fulton Street, as part of the Dutch Reformed Church, was 'not mixed up in questions, controversies and divisions of the day', but others believed that these questions required a response.[13]

In Ulster there was considerable controversy about the social effects of the Revival. It was claimed that there was an

increase in drunkenness, criminal offences and personal mis-
conduct in the north of Ireland during the height of the
Revival, and statistics to this effect were published in the
Northern Whig, and reprinted in *The Times*. Charles Dickens
was one of those who supported the view that there had been
no improvement in society as a result of the Revival.[14] On the
other hand, much evidence was adduced to show that behaviour had improved among revival converts, as well as in the
wider society. The debate raged in Ireland and England for six
months. William Gibson wrote about the levels of crime in
Ulster during the year of the Revival, and reported that the
number of prisoners for trial at the Quarter-Sessions for
County Antrim in October 1859 – that is, six months after the
commencement of the Revival – was exactly half that of the
previous year. At neither the Ballymena nor Londonderry
Quarter-Sessions in April 1860 was there a single case to hear.
Gibson quoted a letter to the Bishop of Down from one of the
clergy in the Diocese, Edward Maguire, who wrote that he had
spoken to three local magistrates who all said that 'public
morals were vastly improved'. In Belfast, it seemed that cases
of drunkenness had increased during the year of revival, but
Gibson's case was based on the fact that none of those before
the police court in Belfast on a charge of drunkenness had, as
he put it, 'ever been brought under religious influences'.[15]

One result of this controversy was that a book was written
by Benjamin Scott, *The Revival in Ulster: Its Moral and Social
Results* (1859), which contained a great deal of evidence of the
way in which the Revival had brought beneficial results to the
wider society. William Arthur, in a letter that *The Times* refused
to print, and which appeared in the *Daily News*, commented:

> During three weeks spent in the midst of the Revival, it was my
> conviction that, after having travelled in the four quarters of the
> world, and used some care to observe moral symptoms, I had
> never witnessed anything to be compared with what I found
> from Coleraine to Belfast, in evidence of a great and sudden
> improvement in the lives of a population . . . My favourite
> informants were not parsons, religious men, or new converts,
> but boys in the street, working-men, car-drivers, policemen,

and strangers, picked up here and there. As to all other things connected with the Revival, I found much difference of opinion; but as to the moral results, none, except that some would ask—will this reformation last?[16]

Henry Venn, the highly respected Anglican evangelical leader, made a tour of the areas of Ireland affected by the Revival and came back with a description of its benefits, including reports of conversations he had held with a range of people who had confirmed that crime had 'exceedingly diminished'.[17]

In Wales, similar evidence in favour of the improved social consequences of the Revival was presented. It was acknowledged that it was legitimate that a revival should be measured by its moral results. After twelve months of revival, a report from Cardiganshire gave the example of those who had been known as drunkards being radically changed. One case was highlighted in which a young man, who was often drunk, boasted that he would not be changed by the Revival, but in less than half an hour after the statement he found himself crying to God for mercy. Another example was a young man who said he would get something to drink, so as to be better able to attack those of his acquaintances who were at revival meetings. He approached the meeting-place and shouted, 'I am Saul of Tarsus coming to persecute you', but before he left the place he became sober and began to cry for mercy.[18] One Welsh minister insisted that 'if it is a religious revival, it will also be a social revival' and the ministers in Wales believed that this was what they were seeing. In the light of the good effects, one of them issued a challenge to anyone who 'knows anything of true religion' to 'deny, that the revival in Ireland and in Wales, is the work of God'.[19]

Communal action

An investigation into the social consequences of the Revival needs to be supplemented by an examination of any communal action that took place as a result. The lives of individuals were clearly affected, and these individuals made an impact in their local communities. However, there were also ways in which the wider body of evangelical Christians became involved in social action. In *The Fervent Prayer*, Edwin Orr devotes two chapters to the 'Social Influence' (his phrase) of the movement of revival. This was the period when the Temperance movement was gaining a strong following among evangelicals and evangelists in North America and across Britain stressed this theme. When Phoebe Palmer was preaching in Newcastle in September 1859, someone who was a member of the Wesleyan Methodist congregation but was a brewer came forward as a result of the appeal and then asked if he could address the meeting. In his statement, he 'referred to the benefit he had received from the services during the week, and publicly declared that the effect of these services on his mind was a resolution to take immediate steps to dissociate himself from the traffic with which he had been connected *and to be done with it for ever*.' This report of the meeting, by Robert Young, a Wesleyan minister, spoke of the effect of this speech as 'electric'.[20]

The message of temperance was not only purveyed by travelling evangelists but also by local ministers. In Eyemouth, in Berwickshire, Scotland, John Turnball, reporting on the effects of the Revival in the town, placed at the head of his list the fact that it had 'introduced and maintained an almost universal temperance'. He acknowledged that many of the fishermen in Eyemouth had been temperate in their use of alcohol but said there was a concern among the ministers in the community – it seems that the United Presbyterian, Baptist and Methodist ministers were particularly involved in the Revival – about several who had been drinking heavily. Turnball was able to report that from the end of November 1859 the pubs had been closed most of the time. He and others had asked all those who had been converted whether they had been in a pub or drunk alcohol since their conversion and many of them had made a statement of this kind: 'Not only have we not tasted strong drink, but we have no desire to do so.' Turnball added one telling incident. It had been necessary to pull a large fishing boat up the shore, and always when this had to be done, at least a hundred and perhaps a hundred and fifty men would come to do the work. In the past they had always been paid in whisky. On this occasion the whisky was provided, the boat was hauled up – and the men went away, leaving the whisky cask with the seal unbroken.[21] The message of temperance had a powerful effect on communities.

Another area of social endeavour was the attempt to reduce levels of prostitution. In London, controversy was sparked off by the efforts that were made to bring the evangelical message to prostitutes in the West End. Midnight meetings, as they were called, were arranged. Meetings were held in different languages since a number of the women were from abroad. Women who wanted to leave prostitution were taken to safe houses. This movement spread to other cities.[22] In Belfast, Hugh Hanna considered that before the Revival, Christians simply ignored the problem of prostitution in the city. The effect of the Revival, however, had been to challenge churches to arrange meetings specifically for those who were victims of prostitution. Hanna was aware of about fifteen women who had left prostitution and found a new life.[23] He wrote later to confirm what he had stated, and his evidence was supplemented by a report from the Episcopalian, Theophilus Campbell, who spoke of women leaving brothels because of the effect of the Revival message.[24] The wider movement to help prostitutes became more organized. By August 1860 a report on the London meetings, which had been addressed by Baptist Noel and Reginald Radcliffe, said that two thousand women had attended (with an average age of twenty-two) and ninety-one had been provided with new homes.[25]

Hugh Hanna's perspective was that the Revival had brought about a series of social changes. He spoke about 'a marked change in the homes of the working classes'. Some of his comments reflected rather blinkered middle-class values, for example, his observation that many of them were 'destitute of any very commendable notions of domestic comfort and taste' but he highlighted the way in which education had become more central. He made a point of visiting evening classes that had opened in working-class areas. About seven hundred and fifty people were present in the classes he visited. As a result of the new 'thirst for education', as Hanna described it, it had been discovered that many more people were illiterate than had previously been thought. Hanna spoke of old men sitting in classes with children, learning to read, and in particular to read the Bible.

Above all, Hanna spoke of the way the Revival had 'exerted the happiest influence' on the relationships between Protestants and Roman Catholics. He wrote: 'The party feuds of Ireland have been exceedingly mischievous. The anniversary of the battle of the Boyne stirred up all the bad blood of the country, and Protestants and Romanists were disposed to engage in bloody strife. But on the last 12th of July there was not a blow struck over all the country.' He argued that 'Love', which he called the fruit of the Revival, had taken the place of 'rankling enmity'.[26]

The question of the effect of the Revival on militant Protestantism, as exemplified in the Orange Order, is a significant one. L.E. Berkley, a minister in Lurgan, where sectarian tensions were evident, spoke of how a young man in his congregation had asked him to give a subscription to the building or providing of an Orange Hall. He had refused, and had incurred the young man's displeasure. However, when the Revival came, the young man told the minister that 'it would be better for everyone to try and serve God Almighty, and let party work alone'. Berkley believed that this opinion was widespread and his view was backed up by H.M. Waddell, who had been a missionary in West Africa, and was commenting on the situation in County Monaghan. A senior Presbyterian elder had told Waddell that 'he saw the power of God in this revival, for nothing else could have put down the Orange Society. Government had failed to suppress it; yet here we see it dying of itself under the influence of revived religion'. Against this background, a Roman Catholic, Chief Baron Pigott, sitting as a judge in County Down, was reported as having said that 'the religious movement in the north' had 'extinguished all party animosities, and produced the most wholesome moral results upon the community at large', and as expressing 'a hope that it would extend over the whole country'.[27]

Across Victorian Britain, the large numbers of orphans constituted another area of social need. One of those who addressed this was Thomas Barnardo. When the Dublin Revival meetings took place, Barnardo, then a teenager, was scornful. He had been influenced by Voltaire and Tom Paine and saw himself as an agnostic. When two of his older brothers were converted, they urged him to go with them to the meetings. Eventually he went to a meeting in a private home where he tried to disrupt what was going on. The gentle approach of the speaker impressed him, however, despite his scepticism. He was converted in 1862 through John Hambledon, and joined a Bible class run by Grattan Guinness. Through this, in 1866, he was introduced to Hudson Taylor.

Barnardo hoped that he might go overseas but while studying medicine in London he was deeply challenged by the conditions of unwanted children in London's East End. He took over a dilapidated cottage, which he opened as a school. At a missionary conference in 1867 Barnardo made a powerful speech about the plight of orphans and Lord Shaftesbury offered to help him establish homes for these children. Other supporters became involved. In 1872, Barnardo purchased a well-known Gin Palace as a centre for his work. By 1878, he had established 50 orphanages.[28] His vision has continued in the form of a major charity, Barnardo's, working on behalf of children. Evangelical concern for orphans was one significant aspect of the renewed evangelical activism of the period.

Mission further afield

The Revival had a powerful impact on mission to places outside the areas in which it was first felt. Henry Venn, the director of the Church Missionary Society, said in 1859 that he was 'anxious to connect the Revival with missionary zeal'. A year later a conference on mission was arranged in Liverpool. Here, Andrew Somerville, the Secretary for Foreign Mission of the United Presbyterian Church, was one of those who spoke about the way in which missionaries 'had heard of these blessed outpourings in North America, in Sweden, in Ireland, in Scotland, in various parts of the metropolis, and other places', and added that they had been coming together –

Anglicans, Dissenters, Baptists, Wesleyans and Presbyterians – to pray 'that God would bless them from day to day'. In connection with this conference, there was a public meeting in Liverpool's Philharmonic Hall and Lord Shaftesbury, as chairman, spoke of this as an 'Ecumenical Council', representing a union for the purpose of mission of 'all evangelical and orthodox denominations'. This historic conference was followed by others – in London in 1888, in New York in 1900, and in Edinburgh in 1910. As Orr argues, the Revival helped to lay the foundations for 'modern international and interdenominational mission'.[29]

Links across Europe were part of the early Revival period, with the involvement of evangelicals in the Scandinavian countries and Germany being particularly evident. Among the other areas in Europe affected by the Revival were parts of Switzerland, France, Belgium and Bohemia. Links between evangelicals in Western Europe and in Russia were made significantly stronger through the work of a prominent British lay evangelical, Granville A.W. Waldegrave – Lord Radstock – whose active involvement in evangelical ministry was shaped in the Revival period. Trotter, his biographer, when writing about one of his early experiences of 'answered prayer', said that this was in 1860.[30] She continued: 'The great spiritual Revival of the sixties in which Lord Radstock became such a moving factor, spread throughout England, Ireland and Scotland and afterwards to the Continent, and he became more and more identified with it.'[31] He had served in the Crimean War and so knew something of the Russian situation. In 1868, he spoke about the evangelical faith to several members of the Russian aristocracy who were in Paris. Radstock spoke fluent French and this was the language of communication. These contacts in Paris led, in the 1870s, to his paying several visits to St Petersburg, the capital of the Russian Empire.

One of Radstock's early contacts was a Russian noblewoman, Elizaveta I. Chertkova. In 1865, her twelve-year-old son died. He had become an evangelical believer under the influence of a tutor, and his final words of testimony left such a deep impression on his mother that she became a seeker after Christ. While abroad she heard Lord Radstock preach and accepted the message he brought. She invited Radstock to visit the Russian capital, and this led to his taking meetings in the houses (often palaces) of leading St Petersburg families. The effect was extraordinary. Several wealthy and influential figures became evangelicals, notably Count Aleksey Bobrinskiy, at one time Russian Minister of Transportation; Count Modest M. Korff, who was in the Royal Court; Princess Vera Lieven; her sister Princess Natalia Gagarina and other members of her family; and Colonel Vasiliy A. Pashkov, a former soldier of the Royal Guard.[32] What was called 'Radstockism' and then 'Pashkovism' became a topic of conversation in Russia.

Others began to come over from England to speak at these 'drawing room revival' meetings, including George Müller. A mansion owned by Pashkov on the Neva in St Petersburg – he had several large estates – became an important meeting place. Up to forty aristocratic homes were at one time open to evangelicals. Pashkov and others began to pass on the message to the workers on their estates, to print and distribute tracts, and to organize Christian philanthropic ventures. The efforts on behalf of the poor, which owed a great deal to women in this circle, included hospital and prison visiting, helping unemployed people find work, and setting up a shelter for homeless children. The Pashkovite movement also contributed to the shaping of the wider movement of Baptists in Russia.[33]

Through Radstock and others, the movement of revival in Britain spread to eastern parts of Europe, and in a similar way the impetus in North America went from the southern states to the Caribbean. In 1858, there were 'gracious outpourings of the Spirit' among Wesleyan Methodists in Barbados and a year later an awakening began in a Moravian congregation in Jamaica. Ernest Payne speaks of this as a 'remarkable spiritual revival', which spread from the south coast and moved across the whole island. Payne continues: 'Chapels became once more crowded. There was widespread conviction of sin. Crime diminished. Men's ethical standards were raised. There was renewed generosity.'[34] Edwin Orr notes that there were also references to 'unhealthy excitement and religious hysteria', but for Orr this was understandable among recently liberated slaves. The revival movement had such a powerful impact that in 1867 the London Missionary Society decided that they no longer needed to have foreign missionaries in Jamaica since the witness of Jamaicans was so effective. In Trinidad, meanwhile, the local Christians developed their own missionary vision.[35]

Revival influences from North America and from Britain spread much farther afield. Lottie Moon, pioneer Southern Baptist missionary to China, was converted during Revival meetings in Charlottesville, Virginia, the church where John A. Broadus was pastor.[36] She went to Cartersville, Georgia, to teach in a new school for girls, and later, when an appeal was given in Cartersville Baptist Church for volunteers to go overseas, Lottie Moon and a colleague responded. In 1873, the Southern Baptist Convention's Foreign Mission Board appointed Lottie Moon to North China.

The 1860s and 1870s saw a whole range of North American mission outreach into China – in addition to the Baptists there were Episcopal, Presbyterian and Methodist initiatives. From Scotland, James Gilmour, who had been converted in 1859, went as far as Mongolia. The China Inland Mission, under Hudson Taylor, became the largest of all the missionary bodies. Taylor's spiritual formation was affected by the Revival. When, in 1860, his friend George Pearse wrote to him to say that 'revival has reached London and hundreds are being converted', Taylor moved to London to become involved in evangelism. Latourette, commenting on these developments, claimed that the large majority of missionaries and supporting bodies were from groups affected by the evangelical awakenings of the period.[37]

Missionaries and mission work in India were also strongly connected with the Revival. It was missionaries in Ludhiana who, in 1860, asked for worldwide prayer for revival. In Calcutta, Alexander Duff, the Church of Scotland's first missionary to India, was instrumental in arranging united prayer meetings involving Anglicans, Baptists and Congregationalists as well as Presbyterians. Another Presbyterian, the American George Bowen (who later became a Methodist), who had gone to Bombay in 1837, was, as Robert Speer put it, 'greatly moved and seemed almost beside himself' as he heard about the

Revival in Ireland. He was filled with the hope that such a work might be seen in India.[38] A Baptist missionary, John Cough, who was converted during the 1858 awakening in Iowa, became the pioneer of a massive Baptist movement in the Telugu-speaking Andhra region of India. Cough began 1869 with a week of prayer, and revival followed.[39]

Among Indian leaders who became powerful figures in this period of revival in India were John Christian Arulappan and Justus Joseph. When Arulappan read about the Revival in North America and Britain, he prayed for a movement of the Spirit in India, and saw a remarkable work of revival in 1860. Eugene Stock wrote: 'Old and young, men and women and children, suddenly seemed crushed by the agony of a deep conviction of sin, and then, as suddenly, seemed to believe in the forgiveness of sins.'[40]

The holiness revival movements of the nineteenth century, which, as we have seen, owed a great deal to the impact of the Revival, also came to emphasize world mission. A number of key figures within Keswick who had been influenced by the Revival of the late 1850s and early 1860s played a part in the development of a wider mission vision at Keswick. Although Keswick was initially cautious about its meetings being taken over by missionary societies, Reginald Radcliffe invited some friends to join him at a missionary prayer meeting at the Convention. Among those who attended was Eugene Stock, Secretary of the Anglican Church Missionary Society (CMS), who had also felt the impact of the 1859 Revival.[41]

Inspired by the ethos of Keswick, a number of Wesleyan holiness leaders launched a Wesleyan equivalent at Southport. It was designed, they said, to 'make more vital the traditional faith of Methodism'. Early speakers included Hugh Price Hughes, who had been converted in 1860 during the Revival in Wales. He came to epitomize the Wesleyan Forward Movement. The Wesleyan holiness movements also led to significant overseas mission, for example, through the work of C.T. Studd in Africa. In North America, A.B. Simpson, a native of Prince Edward Island, who was a convert of the 1858 movement in Canada (he was convicted under the preaching of Grattan Guinness), went on to found the Christian and

Missionary Alliance, which became a worldwide movement emphasizing holiness and mission.[42]

Conclusion

Brian Edwards, writing about changes in society that follow revival, uses language that confirms the idea of rhythms of revival: 'When God comes by his Spirit in revival then society is always aware of it, not only in the changed lives of the Christians and the more radical change in the lives of the converts, but also in the effect that all this has upon the community.' He also refers to the larger context, and to the way in which those affected by revival go on to alter social and political history.[43] There have been those figures, including some of the evangelical leaders of the later nineteenth century in Britain, who have acted as a conscience to the nation. The story of revival and its relationship to social change is, however, a contested one. Some have seen relatively little social impact as a result of the Revival of this period. There seems to be less evidence for an awakened social conscience in North America, although what might have been the outworking of the Revival was brought to a halt by the Civil War. It is the case that some evangelicals involved in revival have given such emphasis to inner spiritual change that they have neglected social responsibility. Yet a concern for the whole person has been seen by many evangelicals to be a necessary part of the Christian calling. This is not only a feature that characterizes periods of revival but is also part of the wider evangelical story. When there is a powerful revival in the churches, however, there is even greater potential for the gospel to affect society. One of the challenges to evangelicals of the story of revival is to bring together a commitment to spiritual renewal and social change.

8

Conclusion

This book has tried to introduce a number of themes that I consider have been important in the rhythms of revival in the period from the later 1850s to the early 1860s – often referred to (rather restrictively, in my view) as the 1859 Revival. Each chapter has focused on a major theme, although inevitably there has been some overlap. Prayer has been central to all revival movements and was particularly evident in the later 1850s. I suggest that prayer should be seen not so much as a prelude to the Revival as an essential component.

The place of pastors in revival, which is often overlooked, has in my view been crucial. This was true from 1857 – the period of the so-called 'leaderless revival'. At the same time, in the Revival examined here, as with other revival movements, a new liberation was evident as lay people, women as well as men, engaged in ministries in new ways. As I have also tried to show, young people have been at the heart of experiences of revival. In terms of the rhythms of revival, those affected when they are young often give a lifetime of effective Christian service. The significance of the Revival in the lives of individuals has been examined, and it has been noted that many individual lives were changed. But revival is also corporate – indeed, primarily corporate – and the Revival studied here transformed the worship and wider life of Christian communities. Revival is not the same as mission, but it issues in mission, as well as – in most cases – social action. I have surveyed some of the questions relating to these issues.

I am sympathetic to those who think that critical questions have to be asked about revival, as is done in some of the essays in *On Revival: A Critical Examination.*[1] Are the effects over-stated? Have we been too ready to look back rather than forward? What about a tendency, as there was in the 1990s – perhaps now less evident – to prophesy that revival was coming? When revival did not come, those who made the prophecies were often very reluctant to say that they had been wrong. Often there has been an attitude of denial – a refusal to face reality. Yet, having said that, the reality is that there are times in the story of the Church that are notable – and should be noted. In January 1858, *The Christian Advocate*, a leading Methodist paper in North America, spoke of how lay brethren (I take this to mean lay people) were eager to witness, many people were responding to invitations in church services, nearly all who came for help were blessed, experiences of God that were enjoyed remained clear, converts were filled with 'holy boldness', faith became a social topic, families engaged in prayer together, testimonies were given nightly in church meetings and conversions were marked by seriousness of purpose.[2] Perhaps the reply might be that these things should always be present in the Church. However, that is not, in reality, the case. Here the idea of rhythms can help. When there is a lessening of these elements, it does not mean that there is no spiritual life. But to know about times when there is greater evidence of power in the Church is, at least to me, an encouragement.

I have not given much attention to theological issues that divided evangelicals in the period I have surveyed. As Orr argues, the transatlantic and, indeed, global movement of revival considered here was to be found among evangelicals who differed on a number of theological issues.[3] It is significant that C.H. Spurgeon, who I have drawn from at various points in this book, when speaking of the eighteenth-century Evangelical Revival, stated that although 'we, as Calvinists, gravely question the accuracy of much that the Wesleyan Methodists zealously advocated', nonetheless, 'the disciples of Wesley', as well as those who followed (the Calvinistic) George Whitefield, 'brought out very clearly and distinctly the vital truths of the gospel of Jesus Christ'.[4] Three years later he spoke warmly of the General (Arminian) Baptists. Spurgeon suggested: 'It may be said that we have gone down to these brethren [General Baptists] quite as much as they have come up to us, and this is very possible; if truth lies in the valley between these two camps, or if it comprehends both, it is well for us to follow it wherever it goes.' Perhaps Spurgeon's associations with Methodists had also affected him: he added that 'if you want a free grace sermon now-a-days, you will be as likely to get it in a Wesleyan chapel as anywhere'.[5]

There were undoubtedly those who did not persevere after the wave of revival passed. However, the picture presented of Scotland in the magazine *The Revival* took into account the temporary as well as the lasting effects of the Revival, and this was probably a balanced picture. This comment was made in 1865:

> The wave of Divine blessing came to us apparently from Ireland four or five years ago . . . It was a very blessed season, perhaps the most extensive in its operation that we have ever known amongst us. But it has, in a great measure, passed away. Still, the fruits remain – living, active, consistent Christians who keep together, cherishing the memory of the time, blessing and praying for its return'.[6]

These are elements in the rhythms of revival. Theodore Cuyler, who had seen revival during his long pastoral ministry, spoke of how 'God always means to be God'. For Cuyler, there were seasons of revival when God 'bestows spiritual blessings'. These came and come 'when he pleases, how he pleases, and where he pleases. We may labour, we may pray, we may "plant", but we must not dictate'. Cuyler had never found in his ministry that arranging 'peculiar measures to produce a revival' was successful.[7]

Edwin Orr suggests that there was a first phase of the Revival of this period, which showed itself in a remarkable movement of prayer. This in itself, he argues, was the means of winning hundreds of thousands of people to Christian faith and commitment. Then he sees a second phase, which was the development of evangelism. The third phase was the training of a new generation of leaders. I do not follow Orr in this rather neat categorization of the developments, but I agree that all these elements were present. I am not convinced by his description of the first stage of the Revival as 'leaderless', and have tried to show the role of ministers and lay leaders.[8]

I hope that renewed attention will be given to this period, since a century and a half later much of what took place has been forgotten. Since then there have been further significant periods of revival, with the non-Western world, or the global South, increasingly being the focus of evangelical advance. The Revival of the late 1850s and early 1860s was not perfect, and it is possible to add more in the way of critical comment to the story I have told here. But even what might be seen as peculiarities are important. They show that revival takes shape as contextual spirituality. Revival always occurs within particular contexts, and the rhythms of revival, although showing commonality, are worked out in unique ways.

Endnotes

1 Spiritual Revival and Quickening

[1] For Lloyd-Jones, see Iain H. Murray, *D. Martyn Lloyd-Jones: The First Forty Years: 1899–1939* (Edinburgh: Banner of Truth Trust, 1982) and *David Martyn Lloyd-Jones: The Fight of Faith 1939–1981* (Edinburgh: Banner of Truth Trust, 1982); John Brencher, *Martyn Lloyd-Jones (1899–1981) and 20th Century Evangelicalism* (Carlisle: Paternoster, 2003).

[2] Erroll Hulse, *Give Him No Rest: A Call to Prayer for Revival* (Darlington: Evangelical Press, 2006).

[3] Brian H. Edwards, *Revival!: A People Saturated with God* (Darlington: Evangelical Press, 1990); R.E. Davies, *I Will Pour Out My Spirit: A History and Theology of Revivals and Evangelical Awakenings* (Tunbridge Wells: Monarch, 1992).

[4] J. Edwin Orr, *The Second Evangelical Awakening in Britain* (London: Marshall, Morgan & Scott, 1949); J. Edwin Orr, *The Fervent Prayer: The Worldwide Impact of the Great Awakening of 1858* (Chicago: Moody Press, 1974). Orr's title, 'second evangelical awakening', has been questioned. Davies describes the period 1857–59 as the 'third evangelical awakening'.

[5] David W. Bebbington, *Evangelicalism in Modern Britain: A History from the 1730s to the 1980s* (London: Routledge, 1995), p. 116.

[6] Davies, *I Will Pour Out My Spirit*, p. 15.

[7] Richard Carwardine, *Transatlantic Revivalism: Popular Evangelicalism in Britain and America, 1790–1865* (Westport: Greenwood Press, 1978, reprinted by Paternoster, 2006), p. 56.

[8] Philip Sheldrake, *A Brief History of Spirituality* (Oxford: Blackwell, 2007), p. 6; cf. Philip Sheldrake, *Spirituality and History: Questions of Interpretation and Method* (London: SPCK/New York: Orbis Books, 1995), pp. 58, 84–6, 167–8.

9   Some have proposed a sharp distinction between revival and revivalism. See Iain H. Murray, R*evival and Revivalism: The Making and Marring of American Evangelicalism, 1750–1858* (Edinburgh: Banner of Truth Trust, 1994).

10   D. Martyn Lloyd-Jones, *Revival: Can We Make It Happen?* (London: Marshall Pickering, 1986), p. 27.

11   Jonathan Edwards, A History of the Work of Redemption, in John F. Wilson (ed.), *Works of Jonathan Edwards*, Vol. 9 (New Haven: Yale University Press, 1989), pp. 143, 457, 460.

12   Eryn White, 'Revival and Renewal Amongst the Eighteenth-Century Welsh Methodists', in Dyfed Wyn Roberts (ed.), *Revival, Renewal and the Holy Spirit: Studies in Evangelical History and Thought* (Milton Keynes: Paternoster, 2009), p. 4.

13   Richard Lovelace, *Dynamics of Spiritual Life: An Evangelical Theology of Renewal* (Downers Grove, Ill.: InterVarsity Press, 1978). This has gone through many reprintings.

14   Kathryn T. Long, *The Revival of 1857–58: Interpreting an American Religious Awakening* (New York: Oxford University Press, 1998), p. 18, cf. pp. 16–25.

15   See Kate Cooper and Jeremy Gregory (eds), *Revival and Resurgence in Christian History: Papers Read at the 2006 Summer Meeting and the 2007 Winter Meeting of the Ecclesiastical Society* (Studies in Church History): 44 (Woodbridge: The Boydell Press, 2008).

16   Lloyd-Jones, *Revival: Can We Make It Happen?*, pp. 72, 79.

17   Edwards, *Revival!*, p. 30.

18   I am indebted to my friend Julian Hardyman, minister of Eden Baptist Church, Cambridge, for this thought.

19   Stuart Piggin, *Firestorm of the Lord: The History of and Prospects for Revival in the Church and the World* (Carlisle: Paternoster, 2000).

20   Although I have reservations about this approach, I would not concur with the view of one critic that Piggin's use of the Bible in this book is 'idiosyncratic, at points irresponsible, and largely unconvincing' (Mark D. Thompson, review, 3 September 2002, http://www.sydneyanglicans.net/life/books/321a/, accessed 28 May 2009).

21   Iain H. Murray, *Pentecost – Today?: The Biblical Basis for Understanding Revival* (Edinburgh: Banner of Truth Trust, 1998), p. 23; cf. George Smeaton, *The Doctrine of the Holy Spirit* (1882, reprinted Edinburgh: Banner of Truth Trust, 1974), pp. 252–3.

22   Nigel Wright, 'Does Revival Quicken or Deaden the Church?', in Andrew Walker and Kristin Aune (eds), *On Revival: A Critical Examination* (Carlisle: Paternoster, 2003), p. 134.

[23] Murray, *Pentecost – Today?*, pp. 8–13, 28–30.

[24] Ian Stackhouse, 'Revivalism, Faddism and the Gospel', in Walker and Aune, *On Revival*, p. 242.

[25] John E. Colwell, *The Rhythm of Doctrine: A liturgical sketch of Christian faith and faithfulness* (Milton Keynes: Paternoster, 2007).

[26] Nigel Wright in Thomas A. Smail, Andrew Walker and Nigel Wright, *Charismatic Renewal* (London: SPCK, 1993), p. 29; cf. Thomas A. Smail, 'When Wright was right', in Pieter J. Lalleman (ed.), *Challenging to Change: Dialogues with a Radical Baptist Theologian* (London: Spurgeon's College, 2009), pp. 163–74.

[27] John Kent, *Holding the Fort: Studies in Victorian Revivalism* (London: Epworth Press, 1978), p. 71.

[28] Janice Holmes, *Religious Revivals in Britain and Ireland, 1859–1905* (Dublin: Irish Academic Press, 2000), p. 169.

[29] John Coffey, 'Democracy and Popular Religion', in Eugenio F. Biagini (ed.), *Citizenship and Community: Liberals, Radicals and Collective Identities in the British Isles, 1865–1931* (Cambridge: CUP, 1996), pp. 97, 119.

[30] David W. Bebbington, 'Revivals, Revivalism and the Baptists', in *Baptistic Theologies*, Vol. 1, No. 1 (2009), pp. 2–11; see Kenneth S. Jeffrey, *When the Lord Walked the Land: The 1858–62 Revival in the North East of Scotland* (Carlisle: Paternoster, 2002), chapter 2, for theories of revivalism.

[31] Noel Gibbard, *On the Wings of the Dove: The International Effects of the 1904–05 Revival* (Bridgend: Bryntirion Press, 2002); see also Noel Gibbard, *Fire on the Altar: A History and Evaluation of the 1904–05 Welsh Revival* (Bridgend: Bryntirion Press, 2006).

[32] Ian M. Randall, '"Days of Pentecostal Overflowing": Baptists and the Shaping of Pentecostalism', in David W. Bebbington (ed.), *The Gospel in the World: Studies in Baptist History and Thought*, Vol. 1 (Carlisle: Paternoster, 2002), pp. 80–104. For an introduction to the Pentecostal story, see W.J. Hollenweger, *Pentecostalism: Origins and Development Worldwide* (Peabody, Mass.: Hendrickson, 1997).

[33] See P. Hocken, *Streams of Renewal* (Carlisle: Paternoster, 1998, rev. ed.). For the impact of this movement within Baptist life, see Douglas McBain, *Fire Over the Waters: Renewal Among Baptists* (London: Darton, Longman & Todd, 1997); cf. Ian M. Randall, 'Baptist Revival and Renewal in the 1960s', in Cooper and Gregory, *Revival and Resurgence in Christian History*, pp. 341–53.

[34] David W. Bebbington, *The Dominance of Evangelicalism: The Age of Spurgeon and Moody* (Nottingham: Inter-Varsity Press, 2005). It should be noted that this series understands evangelicalism to

have been shaped in the eighteenth century. Some writers have challenged this view: see the discussion in Michael A.G. Haykin and Kenneth J. Stewart (eds), *The Emergence of Evangelicalism* (Nottingham: Inter-Varsity Press, 2008).

[35] See Ian M. Randall, *What a Friend We Have in Jesus: The Evangelical Tradition* (London: Darton, Longman & Todd, 2005).

[36] Thomas Phillips, *The Welsh Revival: Its Origin and Development* (Edinburgh: Banner of Truth Trust, 1995, reprint of 1860), pp. 53-4.

2 The Power of Prayer

[1] Kathryn T. Long, *The Revival of 1857–58: Interpreting an American Religious Awakening* (New York: Oxford University Press, 1998), p. 7.

[2] See John Weir, 'London', in William Reid (ed.), *Authentic Records of Revival, Now in Progress in the United Kingdom* (London: James Nisbet & Co., 1860), pp. 420–1.

[3] Samuel I. Prime, *The Power of Prayer* (New York: Scribner, 1858).

[4] Prime, *Power of Prayer*, p. 23.

[5] William C. Conant, *Narratives of Remarkable Conversions and Revival Incidents* (New York: Derby & Jackson, 1858), p. 358.

[6] Prime, *Power of Prayer*, p. 24.

[7] Talbot W. Chambers, *The Noon Prayer Meeting of the North Dutch Church* (New York: Board of Publication, Reformed Protestant Dutch Church, 1858), p. 42.

[8] Conant, *Narratives of Remarkable Conversions*, p. 358; cf. J. Edwin Orr, *The Fervent Prayer: The Worldwide Impact of the Great Awakening of 1858* (Chicago: Moody Press, 1974), chapter 2.

[9] *Journal of Commerce*, 26 November 1857, cited in Long, *The Revival of 1857–58*, p. 52.

[10] Long, *The Revival of 1857–58*, p. 36.

[11] Janice Holmes, *Religious Revivals in Britain and Ireland, 1859–1905* (Dublin: Irish Academic Press, 2000), p. 4.

[12] William Gibson, *The Year of Grace: A History of the Ulster Revival of 1859* (Edinburgh: Andrew Elliott, 1860).

[13] Gibson, *Year of Grace*, p. 16.

[14] Holmes, *Religious Revivals*, p. 31. Janice Holmes does not deal with Gibson's role as a primary narrator of the Revival.

[15] John Weir, *The Ulster Awakening: Its Origin, Progress, and Fruit* (London: Arthur Hall, Virtue & Co., 1860), pp. 17–18, quoting Samuel Moore.

[16] Gibson, *Year of Grace*, pp. 20–3.

[17] Weir, *Ulster Awakening*, pp. 20–2, quoting an account by William Arthur.

[18] Kenneth S. Jeffrey, *When the Lord Walked the Land: The 1858–62 Revival in the North East of Scotland* (Carlisle: Paternoster, 2002), pp. 55–7; cf. Kenneth S. Jeffrey, 'Making Sense of the 1859 Revival in the North-East of Scotland', in Andrew Walker and Kristin Aune (eds), *On Revival: A Critical Examination* (Carlisle: Paternoster, 2003), p. 106.

[19] J. Barbour Johnstone, 'What hath God wrought', in Reid, *Authentic Records of Revival*, p. 123.

[20] Horatius Bonar, 'Preface', in Reid, *Authentic Records of Revival*, p. iv.

[21] D.W. Roberts, 'The Effect of Charles Finney's Revivalism on the 1858–60 Awakening in Wales', in Dyfed Wyn Roberts (ed.), *Revival, Renewal and the Holy Spirit: Studies in Evangelical History and Thought* (Milton Keynes: Paternoster, 2009) pp. 40–1.

[22] Thomas Phillips, *The Welsh Revival: Its Origin and Development* (Edinburgh: Banner of Truth Trust, 1995, reprint of 1860), pp. 7–8.

[23] Charles Haddon Spurgeon, 'Preface', *The New Park Street Pulpit*, Vol. 5 (1859), (London: Passmore & Alabaster, 1894), p. v.

[24] Conant, *Narratives of Remarkable Conversions*, pp. 380–2.

[25] *New York Daily Tribune*, 11 March 1858, cited by Long, *The Revival of 1857–58*, p. 83.

[26] See Curtis D. Johnson, *Redeeming America: Evangelicals and the Road to Civil War* (Chicago: Ivan R. Dee, 1993), pp. 7–9.

[27] Long, *The Revival of 1857–58*, p. 17.

[28] Mark A. Noll, *America's God: From Jonathan Edwards to Abraham Lincoln* (Oxford: Oxford University Press, 2000), p. 176.

[29] Gibson, *Year of Grace*, pp. 111–13.

[30] Long, *The Revival of 1857–58*, p. 105.

[31] Prime, *Power of Prayer*, pp. 70–3.

[32] Prime, *Power of Prayer*, pp. 73–82.

[33] *Christian Advocate and Journal*, 15 April 1858, cited by Long, *The Revival of 1857–58*, p. 108.

[34] Prime, *Power of Prayer*, pp. 58–60.

[35] *Evangelical Christendom*, October 1859, p. 368; cf. David Hilborn and Ian M. Randall, *One Body in Christ: The History and Significance of the Evangelical Alliance* (Carlisle: Paternoster, 2001), pp. 108–9.

[36] Weir, *Ulster Awakening*, pp. 151–3.

[37] C.H. Spurgeon, 'A Revival Sermon', *The New Park Street Pulpit*, Vol. 6, 1860 (London: Banner of Truth Trust, 1964), p. 84.

38 Spurgeon, 'A Revival Sermon', p. 84.
39 Spurgeon, 'A Revival Sermon', p. 87.
40 Weir, *Ulster Awakening*, p. 113.
41 J. Edwin Orr, *The Second Evangelical Awakening in Britain* (London: Marshall, Morgan & Scott, 1949), pp. 156–7.
42 Orr, *Second Evangelical Awakening*, p. 72.
43 *United Presbyterian Magazine*, Vol. 4 (1860), p. 326.
44 Phillips, *Welsh Revival*, p. 84.
45 Phillips, *Welsh Revival*, p. 84.
46 See Michael A.G. Haykin, *One Heart and One Soul: John Sutcliff of Olney, His Friends and His Times* (Darlington: Evangelical Press, 1994).
47 George Ernest Morgan, '*A Veteran in Revival': R.C. Morgan: His Life and Times* (London: Morgan & Scott, 1909), p. 97.
48 Phillips, *Welsh Revival*, p. 53.
49 Orr, *Second Evangelical Awakening*, p. 263.
50 Holmes, *Religious Revivals in Britain and Ireland*, p. 30.
51 Reviews of 'Recent Publications on Religious Revivals', in *The Baptist Magazine*, August 1859, p. 499.
52 *Report Presented to the Fourteenth Annual Conference, held in Nottingham, October 1860* (London: Evangelical Alliance, 1861), p. 7.
53 *Evangelical Christendom*, August 1860, p. 447; Hilborn and Randall, *One Body in Christ*, pp. 140–2.
54 For this, see Orr, *Fervent Prayer*, pp. 83–5. For more on Sweden and Norway, see M.W. Montgomery, *A Wind from the Holy Spirit in Sweden and Norway* (New York: American Home Missionary Society, 1884).
55 Orr, *Fervent Prayer*, pp. 95–8.
56 Phillips, *Welsh Revival*, p. 3.
57 Phillips, *Welsh Revival*, p. 3.
58 See www.24-7prayer.com
59 Brian H. Edwards, *Revival!: A People Saturated with God* (Darlington: Evangelical Press, 1990), pp. 78–80.

3 The Role of Ministers

1 Thomas Phillips, *The Welsh Revival: Its Origin and Development* (Edinburgh: Banner of Truth Trust, 1995, reprint of 1860), pp. 133–4.
2 Theodore L. Cuyler, *Stirring the Eagle's Nest* (London: James Nisbet & Co., 1892), pp. 301–2.

3   Cuyler, *Stirring the Eagle's Nest*, pp. 302–3; cf. J. Edwin Orr, *The Fervent Prayer: The Worldwide Impact of the Great Awakening of 1858* (Chicago: Moody Press, 1974), p. 113.

4   Theodore L. Cuyler, *How to be a Pastor* (London: James Nisbet & Co., 1891), p. 88.

5   Phillips, *Welsh Revival*, p. 10.

6   Phillips, *Welsh Revival*, pp. 123–4. The minister was T. Edwards.

7   See Kenneth S. Jeffrey, *When the Lord Walked the Land: The 1858–62 Revival in the North East of Scotland* (Carlisle: Paternoster, 2002), pp. 116, 125, 128. The comments by Dower are in T.T. Matthews (ed.), *Reminiscences of the Revival of Fifty-Nine, and the Sixties* (Aberdeen, 1910), p. 119.

8   John Weir, *The Ulster Awakening: Its Origin, Progress, and Fruit* (London: Arthur Hall, Virtue & Co., 1860), pp. 26–7.

9   C.H. Spurgeon, 'What is a Revival?', in *The Sword and the Trowel*, December 1866, p. 532.

10   Francis Wayland and Herman Lincoln Wayland, *A Memoir of the Life and Labors of Francis Wayland*, Vol. 2 (New York: Sheldon, 1867), pp. 213–15.

11   *Watchman and Reflector*, 25 March 1858, cited in Kathryn T. Long, *The Revival of 1857–58: Interpreting an American Religious Awakening* (New York: Oxford University Press, 1998), p. 59.

12   Weir, *Ulster Awakening*, p. 51.

13   David Hempton and Myrtle Hill, *Evangelical Protestantism in Ulster Society, 1740–1890* (London: Routledge, 1992), p. 148.

14   William Gibson, *The Year of Grace: A History of the Ulster Revival of 1859* (Edinburgh: Andrew Elliott, 1860), p. 97.

15   Isaac Nelson, *The Year of Delusion* (Belfast: Mayne, 1860).

16   I consider that Janice Holmes overstates the tension, although she utilizes valuable material: Janice Holmes, *Religious Revivals in Britain and Ireland, 1859–1905* (Dublin: Irish Academic Press, 2000), pp. 8–9.

17   Weir, *Ulster Awakening*, pp. 189–90.

18   See Edwin Orr, *The Fervent Prayer: The Worldwide Impact of the Great Awakening of 1858* (Chicago: Moody Press, 1974), pp. 46, 51, for the involvement of Bishop Knox.

19   J. Edwin Orr, *The Second Evangelical Awakening in Britain* (London: Marshall, Morgan & Scott, 1949), pp. 66–7; Orr, *Fervent Prayer*, chapter 8.

20   Wayland and Wayland, *Life and Labors of Francis Wayland*, pp. 216–19.

21   Phillips, *Welsh Revival*, pp. 29–30.

22 Gibson, *Year of Grace*, p. 112.
23 Orr, *Fervent Prayer*, chapter 17.
24 *The Revival*, 25 August 1860, cited by Orr, *Second Evangelical Awakening*, p. 62.
25 H.C.G. Moule, *Memories of a Vicarage* (London: Religious Tract Society, 1913), pp. 48–9.
26 Ralph Pite, *Thomas Hardy: The Guarded Life* (New Haven: Yale University Press, 2007), pp. 79–85.
27 C.H. Spurgeon, 'Thanksgiving and Prayer', *Metropolitan Tabernacle Pulpit*, Vol. 9 (1863) (Pasadena: Pilgrim Publications, 1969), p. 551.
28 *Annual Paper Concerning the Lord's Work in Connection with the Pastors' College*, 1870 [*Annual Paper*], pp. 5–6. The Pastors' College was later known as Spurgeon's College.
29 Charles Haddon Spurgeon, 'Grieving the Holy Ghost', in *The New Park Street Pulpit*, Vol. 5 (1859), (London: Passmore & Alabaster, 1894), pp. 431–2.
30 *The Lancet*, 23 July 1859, p. 94.
31 Gibson, *Year of Grace*, p. 27.
32 Gibson, *Year of Grace*, pp. 27–8.
33 *Evangelical Christendom*, October 1859, pp. 368–9.
34 Gibson, *Year of Grace*, pp. 221–2.
35 James McCosh, *Christianity and Positivism: A Series of Lectures to the Times on Natural Theology and Christian Apologetics* (London: Macmillan, 1871). He later built on this in a paper, 'Religious Aspects of the Doctrine of Development' – 'development' meaning 'evolution' – arguing that theistic design and Darwin's 'natural law' were compatible. He noted that it was pointless to tell younger naturalists that there were no grounds for the theory of evolution. Despite its problems, he said, 'they know that there is truth [in it], which is not to be set aside by denunciation'. He suggested that 'religious philosophers might be more profitably employed in showing them the religious aspects of the doctrine of development', see James McCosh, 'Religious Aspects of the Doctrine of Development', in Philip Schaff and Samuel Irenaeus Prime (eds.), *History, Essays, Orations and Other Documents of the Sixth General Conference of the Evangelical Alliance* (New York: Harper Row, 1874), pp. 264–71. It is noteworthy that this volume was edited by Prime, who wrote on the Revival in the USA.
36 Phillips, *Welsh Revival*, p. 128.
37 From a correspondent in the *Welsh Standard*, reproduced in Phillips, *Welsh Revival*, pp. 70–1.

[38] George A. Blackburn (ed.), *The Life and Work of John L. Girardeau* (Columbia, S.C.: The State Co., 1916), pp. 99–100.

[39] C.H. Spurgeon, 'Characteristics of Faith', *The New Park Street Pulpit*, Vol. 6 (1860), p. 250.

[40] C.H. Spurgeon, 'A Sermon for the Week of Prayer', *New Park Street Pulpit and Metropolitan Tabernacle Pulpit*, Vol. 7 (1861) (Pasadena: Pilgrim Publications, 1969), p. 389.

[41] *Evangelical Christendom* (1860), pp. 602–7.

[42] Phillips, *Welsh Revival*, p. 11.

[43] Phillips, *Welsh Revival*, p. 11.

[44] Orr, *Second Evangelical Awakening*, p. 89.

[45] J.J. Morgan, *The '59 Revival in Wales: Some Incidents in the Life and Work of David Morgan, Ysbytty* (Mold: J.J. Morgan, 1909), pp. 117–21.

[46] Hempton and Hill, *Evangelical Protestantism in Ulster Society*, p. 151.

[47] Gibson, *Year of Grace*, p. 206.

[48] See Hylson-Smith, *Evangelicals in the Church of England* (Edinburgh: T&T Clark, 1989), p. 183.

[49] *Annual Paper*, 1891–92, p. 12; M. Nicholls, *C.H. Spurgeon: The Pastor Evangelist* (Didcot: Baptist Historical Society), p. 99.

[50] *The Sword and the Trowel*, January 1866, pp. 41–3.

[51] *Annual Paper*, 1870, p. 7; cf. David W. Bebbington, 'Spurgeon and the Common Man', *Baptist Review of Theology*, Vol. 5, No. 1 (1995), pp. 63–75.

[52] Brian H. Edwards, *Revival!: A People Saturated with God* (Darlington: Evangelical Press, 1990), pp. 271–5.

4 Emerging Evangelists

[1] J. Edwin Orr, *The Second Evangelical Awakening in Britain* (London: Marshall, Morgan & Scott, 1949), pp. 230–1.

[2] Orr, *Second Evangelical Awakening*, p. 231.

[3] See Carwardine, *Transatlantic Revivalism*, chapter 6, and, recently, Nigel Scotland, *Apostles of the Spirit and Fire: American Revivalists and Victorian Britain* (Milton Keynes: Paternoster, 2009), chapters 4 and 5.

[4] Orr, *Second Evangelical Awakening*, pp. 232–3.

[5] David Bundy, 'The Legacy of William Taylor', *International Bulletin of Missionary Research*, October 1994, pp. 172–6.

[6] William Taylor, *Christian Adventures in South Africa* (New York: Nelson & Phillips, 1876), pp. 2–3, 94–8, 451; cf. David Hempton,

Methodism: Empire of the Spirit (New Haven: Yale University Press, 2005), p. 172.

7   Melvin E. Dieter, *The Holiness Revival of the Nineteenth Century* (Metuchen, N.J.: Scarecrow Press, 1980), pp. 26–45.

8   Orr, *Fervent Prayer*, pp. 2–3.

9   *The Times*, 21 September 1859, p. 10.

10 Orr, *Second Evangelical Awakening*, pp. 127, 137. Janice Holmes suggests that what happened in Newcastle never spread beyond that region (Janice Holmes, *Religious Revivals in Britain and Ireland, 1859–1905* (Dublin: Irish Academic Press, 2000), pp. 36–7) but this does not seem to be the case.

11 Scotland, *Apostles of the Spirit and Fire*, p. 127.

12 K. Moody-Stuart, *Brownlow North: Records and Recollections* (London: Hodder & Stoughton, 1878), pp. 25, 286.

13 Jane Radcliffe, *Recollections of Reginald Radcliffe* (London: Morgan & Scott, 1896), p. 136.

14 Orr, *Second Evangelical Awakening*, p. 121.

15 The story of the Open Brethren is told in Tim Grass, *Gathering to His Name: The Story of the Brethren in Britain and Ireland* (Carlisle: Paternoster, 2006).

16 Neil T.R. Dickson, *Brethren in Scotland, 1838–2000* (Carlisle: Paternoster, 2002), p. 73; cf. Radcliffe, *Recollections*, pp. 71–4.

17 George Ernest Morgan, *A Veteran in Revival: R.C. Morgan, His Life and Times* (London: Morgan & Scott, 1909), p. 21.

18 W.J. Brealey, *'Always Abounding'; or Recollections of the Life and Labours of the late George Brealey, the Evangelist of the Blackdown Hills* (London: Shaw and Co, 2nd ed., 1889), p. 51.

19 Henry Varley Jr., *Henry Varley's Life Story* (London: Alfred Holness, 1916), p. 74.

20 William Blair, 'The things which we have seen and heard', in William Reid (ed.), *Authentic Records of Revival, Now in Progress in the United Kingdom* (London: James Nisbet & Co., 1860), p. 56.

21 John Weir, 'London', in Reid, *Authentic Records of Revival*, p. 428.

22 N.T.R. Dickson, 'Revivalism and the Limits of Cooperation: Brethren Origins in Orkney in the 1860s', in Neil T.R. Dickson and Tim Grass (eds.), *The Growth of the Brethren Movement: National and International Experiences* (Carlisle: Paternoster, 2006), pp. 80–91; Dickson, *Brethren in Scotland*, pp. 83–4.

23 Orr, *Second Evangelical Awakening*, pp. 69–70.

24 David W. Bebbington, 'Revival and the Clash of Cultures: Ferryden, Forfarshire in 1859', in Dyfed Wyn Roberts (ed.),

Revival, Renewal and the Holy Spirit: Studies in Evangelical History and Thought (Milton Keynes: Paternoster, 2009), pp. 65–94.

[25] Kenneth S. Jeffrey, *When the Lord Walked the Land: The 1858–62 Revival in the North East of Scotland* (Carlisle: Paternoster, 2002), p. 187.

[26] *Peterhead Sentinel*, 30 March 1860, p. 2, cited by Jeffrey, *When the Lord Walked the Land*, p. 192.

[27] Jeffrey, *When the Lord Walked the Land*, p. 216.

[28] Orr, *Second Evangelical Awakening*, p. 157; John Kent, *Holding the Fort: Studies in Victorian Revivalism* (London: Epworth Press, 1978), pp. 111–13.

[29] William Gibson, *The Year of Grace: A History of the Ulster Revival of 1859* (Edinburgh: Andrew Elliott, 1860), pp. 66–7.

[30] Donald M. Lewis, *Lighten their Darkness: The Evangelical Mission to Working-class London, 1828–1860* (Carlisle: Paternoster, 2001).

[31] For the wider picture, see Hugh McLeod, *Religion and Society in England, 1850–1914* (Basingstoke: Macmillan, 1996).

[32] Holmes, *Religious Revivals in Britain and Ireland*, pp. 135–8, p. 141.

[33] A life of Richard Weaver was written by James Paterson, of White Memorial Free Church, Glasgow: James Paterson, *Richard Weaver's Life Story* (London: Morgan & Scott, 1897); cf. Holmes, *Religious Revivals in Britain and Ireland*, p. 138.

[34] Orr, *Second Evangelical Awakening*, p. 160.

[35] Holmes, *Religious Revivals in Britain and Ireland*, pp. 148–9.

[36] *The Revival* reported on the events in Nottingham throughout 1864 and 1865. For a summary, see Orr, *Second Evangelical Awakening*, pp. 138–44.

[37] *The Revival*, 23 February 1861, p. 61.

[38] Holmes, *Religious Revivals in Britain and Ireland*, pp. 149–52.

[39] C.M. Birrell, 'The Lessons of Recent Revivals of Religion', *Baptist Magazine*, September 1860, p. 563.

[40] Frederick B. Meyer, *The Bells of Is: Or Voices of Human Need and Sorrow* (London: S.W. Partridge, 1902), pp. 18–19; cf. Ian M. Randall, *Spirituality and Social Change: The Contribution of F.B. Meyer (1847–1929)*, (Carlisle: Paternoster, 2003), chapter 2.

[41] *The Christian*, 14 August 1873, p. 8.

[42] For a discussion, see Amanda Vickery, 'Golden Age to Separate Spheres? A Review of the Categories and Chronology of English Women's History', in *The Historical Journal*, Vol. 36, No. 2 (1993), pp. 383–414.

[43] Frank K. Prochaska, 'Body and Soul: Bible Nurses and the Poor in Victorian London', *Historical Review*, Vol. 60 (1987), pp. 336–48.

44 E.D. Graham, 'Chosen by God: The Female Travelling Preachers of Early Primitive Methodism', in Tim Macquiban (ed.), *Methodism in its Cultural Milieu, Westminster Wesley Series*, No. 2 (Cambridge: Applied Theology Press, 1994), pp. 85–98.

45 *The Sword and the Trowel*, January 1865, p. 31.

46 Danzy Sheen, *Pastor C.H. Spurgeon: His Conversion, Career and Coronation* (London: J.B. Knapp, 1892), p. 80.

47 Phoebe Palmer, *Promise of the Father: Or, a Neglected Spirituality of the Last Days* (Boston: H.V. Degan, 1859); Margaret H. McFadden, *Golden Cables of Sympathy: The Transatlantic Sources of Nineteenth-Century Feminism* (Lexington, Ky.: University Press of Kentucky, 2009), p. 53; Kathryn T. Long, *The Revival of 1857–58: Interpreting an American Religious Awakening* (New York: Oxford University Press, 1998), pp. 49–50.

48 Phoebe Palmer, *The Tongue of Fire on the Daughters of the Lord: Or, Questions in Relation to the Duty of the Christian Church in Regard to the Privileges of Her Female Membership* (New York: W.C. Palmer, Jr., 1869).

49 Holmes, *Religious Revivals in Britain and Ireland*, p. 110.

50 Brian H. Edwards, *Revival!: A People Saturated with God* (Darlington: Evangelical Press, 1990), p. 207.

51 For Hooper, see Fanny Guinness, *'She Spake of Him': Being Recollections of the Loving Labours and Early Death of the late Mrs Henry Dening* (Bristol: W. Mack, 1872).

52 William Haslam, *Yet not I: Or More Years of Ministry* (London: Morgan & Scott, 1882), p. 163.

53 Olive Anderson, 'Women preachers in mid-Victorian Britain: Some reflections on feminism, popular religion and social change', in *Historical Journal*, Vol. 12 (1969), p. 477.

54 David W. Bebbington, *Evangelicalism in Modern Britain: A History from the 1730s to the 1980s* (London: Routledge, 1995), p. 159.

55 Holmes, *Religious Revivals in Britain and Ireland*, pp. 116–19.

56 Neil T.R. Dickson, *Brethren in Scotland, 1838–2000* (Carlisle: Paternoster Press, 2002), pp. 74–7.

57 Norman H. Murdoch, 'Female Ministry in the Thought and Work of Catherine Booth', *Church History*, Vol. 53, No. 3 (1984), pp. 348–62.

58 Anderson, 'Women preachers', pp. 480–1.

59 *War Cry*, 4 September 1886, p. 1.

60 Holmes, *Religious Revivals in Britain and Ireland*, pp. 120–1.

61 Typewritten obituary of Annie Davies, cited in Holmes, *Religious Revivals in Britain and Ireland*, p. 121.

[62] Holmes, *Religious Revivals in Britain and Ireland*, pp. 124–5.

[63] Charles Price and Ian M. Randall, *Transforming Keswick: The Keswick Convention Past, Present and Future* (Carlisle: Paternoster/OM Publishing, 2000), pp. 21–31; John C. Pollock, *The Keswick Story* (Fort Washington, Penn.: CLC, 2006, reprint), pp. 41–50; Dieter, *Holiness Revival*, pp. 159–69.

[65] Samuel I. Prime, *The Power of Prayer* (New York: Scribner, 1858), pp. 60–1.

[66] Prime, *Power of Prayer*, pp. 60–2.

5 Youth Taking Part

[1] Kathryn T. Long, *The Revival of 1857–58: Interpreting an American Religious Awakening* (New York: Oxford University Press, 1998), p. 129.

[2] Delavan Leonard Pierson, *A.T. Pierson: A Biography* (London: James Nisbet & Co., 1912), pp. 66–7, 130.

[3] William C. Conant, *Narratives of Remarkable Conversions and Revival Incidents* (New York: Derby & Jackson, 1858), pp. 399–400, 413–14.

[4] Conant, *Narratives of Remarkable Conversions*, p. 436.

[5] Don Sweeting, 'The Great Turning Point in the Life of D.L. Moody', in Timothy George (ed.), *Mr Moody and the Evangelical Tradition* (London and New York: T&T Clark, 2004), p. 40.

[6] John Weir, 'London', in William Reid (ed.), *Authentic Records of Revival, Now in Progress in the United Kingdom* (London: James Nisbet & Co., 1860), pp. 408–10.

[7] Weir, 'London', pp. 411–12.

[8] Weir, 'London', pp. 412–14.

[9] Thomas Phillips, *The Welsh Revival: Its Origin and Development* (Edinburgh: Banner of Truth Trust, 1995, reprint of 1860), pp. 47–8.

[10] Phillips, *Welsh Revival*, p. 20.

[11] Brian Stanley, *The History of the Baptist Missionary Society, 1792–1992* (Edinburgh: T&T Clark, 1992), pp. 180–1.

[12] J. Edwin Orr, *The Second Evangelical Awakening in Britain* (London: Marshall, Morgan & Scott, 1949), pp. 118–19, citing *The Nonconformist*, 30 November 1859 and *The Record*, 5 December 1859.

[13] For Aitken, see Charlotte E. Woods, *Memoirs and Letters of Canon Hay Aitken* (London: C.W. Daniel, 1928).

[14] D. Johnson, *Contending for the Faith* (Leicester: Inter-Varsity Press, 1979), p. 57.

15 Orr, *Second Evangelical Awakening*, p. 74.

16 Orr, *Second Evangelical Awakening*, p. 56.

17 Archibald T. Robertson, *Life and Letters of John A. Broadus* (Philadelphia: American Baptist Publication Society, 1901), p. 134.

18 Long, *The Revival of 1857–58*, pp. 62–3. In 1893 Briggs was put out of his position in the Presbyterian Church because of his embrace of biblical criticism.

19 Long, *The Revival of 1857–58*, pp. 63–4; Bradley J. Longfield, 'From Evangelicalism to Liberalism: Public Midwestern Universities in Nineteenth-Century America', in George M. Marsden and Bradley J. Longfield (eds.), *The Secularization of the Academy* (New York: Oxford University Press, 1992), p. 54.

20 Timothy L. Smith, *Revivalism and Social Reform: American Protestantism on the Eve of the Civil War* (Nashville: Abingdon Press, 1957), pp. 100–2, 159.

21 Conant, *Narratives of Remarkable Conversions*, p. 378.

22 William Jeynes, *Religion, Education and Academic Success* (Greenwich, Conn.: Information Age, 2003), p. 68.

23 Prime, *Power of Prayer*, pp. 170–1.

24 John Weir, *The Ulster Awakening: Its Origin, Progress, and Fruit* (London: Arthur Hall, Virtue & Co., 1860), pp. 146–7.

25 James Bain, 'Straid', in Reid, *Authentic Records of Revival*, pp. 149,150.

26 Phillips, *Welsh Revival*, pp. 35–6.

27 Phillips, *Welsh Revival*, p. 52.

28 Phillips, *Welsh Revival*, p. 52.

29 Harry Sprange, *Kingdom Kids: The Story of Scotland's Children in Revival* (Fearn: Christian Focus, 1994).

30 Sprange, *Kingdom Kids*, p. 11. He is following the view of D.A. Currie, 'The Growth of Evangelicals in the years 1793–1843' (St Andrews University, PhD thesis, 1990), p. 358.

31 Sprange, *Kingdom Kids*, p. 169.

32 George Stevenson, 'Pulteneytown, Wick', in William Reid (ed.), *Authentic Records of Revival, Now in Progress in the United Kingdom* (London: James Nisbet & Co., 1860), pp. 445–6. The town of Wick was my birthplace.

33 *The Revival*, 5 March 1863. See comment in Sprange, *Kingdom Kids*, pp. 176–87.

34 James Morgan, 'Fisherwick Place Church, Belfast', in Reid (ed.), *Authentic Records of Revival*, p. 14.

35 Weir, *Ulster Awakening*, p. 66.

36 Francis Wayland and Herman Lincoln Wayland, *A Memoir of the Life and Labors of Francis Wayland*, Vol. 2 (New York: Sheldon, 1867), p. 213.

[37] See Neil Summerton, 'George Müller and the Financing of the Scriptural Knowledge Institution', in Neil T.R. Dickson and Tim Grass (eds.), *The Growth of the Brethren Movement* (Carlisle: Paternoster, 2006), pp. 49–79.

[38] Arthur T. Pierson, *George Mueller of Bristol* (London: J. Nisbet & Co., 1899), chapter 23.

[39] Nigel Scotland, *Apostles of the Spirit and Fire: American Revivalists and Victorian Britain* (Milton Keynes: Paternoster, 2009), pp. 165–6.

[40] Scotland, *Apostles of the Spirit and Fire*, pp. 170–1.

[41] Orr, *Fervent Prayer*, p. 116.

[42] For Operation Mobilisation (OM) see Ian M. Randall, *Spiritual Revolution: The Story of OM* (Milton Keynes: Authentic Media, 2008).

6 Church Renewal

[1] Thomas Phillips, *The Welsh Revival: Its Origin and Development* (Edinburgh: Banner of Truth Trust, 1995, reprint of 1860), p. 12.

[2] Taken from William C. Conant, *Narratives of Remarkable Conversions and Revival Incidents* (New York: Derby & Jackson, 1858), pp. 417–23.

[3] Thomas Toye, 'Great St George's Street, Belfast', in William Reid (ed.), *Authentic Records of Revival, Now in Progress in the United Kingdom* (London: James Nisbet & Co., 1860), pp. 113–15.

[4] Kenneth S. Jeffrey, *When the Lord Walked the Land: The 1858–62 Revival in the North East of Scotland* (Carlisle: Paternoster, 2002), pp. 116, 118, 128, 130, 174, citing *A Report of a Conference on the State of Religion and Public Meeting, held in the Free Church, Huntly, January 5, 1860* (Huntly, 1860).

[5] Phillips, *Welsh Revival*.

[6] Phillips, *Welsh Revival*, pp. 79–80.

[7] Thomas Henson, *Centennial Memorials of the Baptist Church in Earl's Colne* (Earl's Colne, 1886), pp. 12–14.

[8] Samuel I. Prime, *The Power of Prayer* (New York: Scribner, 1858), pp. 71–2.

[9] Prime, *Power of Prayer*, pp. 132, 204.

[10] Phillips, *Welsh Revival*, p. 35.

[11] Thomas Toye, 'Great St George's Street, Belfast', in William Reid (ed.), *Authentic Records of Revival, Now in Progress in the United Kingdom* (London: James Nisbet & Co., 1860), pp. 114–15.

[12] J. Denham Smith, 'Times of Refreshing', in Reid (ed.), *Authentic Records of Revival*, pp. 315–17.

13 J. Edwin Orr, *The Second Evangelical Awakening in Britain* (London: Marshall, Morgan & Scott, 1949), p. 95.

14 Orr, *Second Evangelical Awakening*, p. 261.

15 William C. Conant, *Narratives of Remarkable Conversions and Revival Incidents* (New York: Derby & Jackson, 1858), pp. 397–8.

16 Conant, *Narratives of Remarkable Conversions*, p. 399.

17 See William L. de Arteaga, *Forgotten Power: The Significance of the Lord's Supper in Revival* (Grand Rapids, Mich.: Zondervan, 2002).

18 Phillips, *Welsh Revival*, pp. 12–14.

19 John Weir, *The Ulster Awakening: Its Origin, Progress, and Fruit* (London: Arthur Hall, Virtue & Co., 1860), p. 21.

20 Kenneth S. Jeffrey, *When the Lord Walked the Land: The 1858–62 Revival in the North East of Scotland* (Carlisle: Paternoster, 2002), p. 134.

21 Tim Grass, *Gathering to His Name: The Story of the Brethren in Britain and Ireland* (Carlisle: Paternoster, 2006), pp. 117–20; Dickson, *Brethren in Scotland*, p. 83.

22 *The Sword and the Trowel*, July 1869, p. 301.

23 C.H. Spurgeon, 'The Lord's Supper', *Metropolitan Tabernacle Pulpit*, Vol. 50 (1861) (Pasadena: Pilgrim Publications, 1978), p. 101.

24 C.H. Spurgeon, 'The Witness of the Lord's Supper', *Metropolitan Tabernacle Pulpit*, Vol. 59 (undated sermon) (Pasadena: Pilgrim Publications, 1979), p. 38.

25 C.H. Spurgeon, 'The Lord's Supper, Simple but Sublime', *Metropolitan Tabernacle Pulpit*, Vol. 55 (1866) (Pasadena: Pilgrim Publications, 1979), pp. 316, 318.

26 Horton Davies, *Worship and Theology in England, Vol. 1: From Cranmer to Hooker 1534–1603* (London: Oxford University Press, 1961), p. 223.

27 Nigel Scotland, *Evangelical Anglicans in a Revolutionary Age, 1789–1901*, (Milton Keynes: Paternoster, 2003), pp. 352–4.

28 Edwin Hodder, *The Life and Work of the Seventh Earl of Shaftesbury, KG* (London: Cassell & Co., 1888), p. 743.

29 Orr, *Second Evangelical Awakening*, pp. 36, 193–8.

30 Edwin Orr, *The Fervent Prayer: The Worldwide Impact of the Great Awakening of 1858* (Chicago: Moody Press, 1974), p. 92.

31 William C. Conant, *Narratives of Remarkable Conversions and Revival Incidents* (New York: Derby & Jackson, 1858), p. 425.

32 Kent, *Holding the Fort*, p. 71.

33 Conant, *Narratives of Remarkable Conversions*, p. 80.

34 Eugene Stock, *My Recollections* (London: James Nisbet & Co., 1909), pp. 82–3.

[35] Orr, *Fervent Prayer*, p. 40.
[36] William Gibson, *The Year of Grace: A History of the Ulster Revival of 1859* (Edinburgh: Andrew Elliott, 1860), pp. 404–29.
[37] Orr, *Second Evangelical Awakening*, pp. 200–1.
[38] Orr, *Fervent Prayer*, pp. 41–2.
[39] J.H.Y. Briggs, *The English Baptists of the Nineteenth Century* (Didcot: Baptist Historical Society, 1994), pp. 300–1. For the theatre services, see Chapter 7.
[40] *The Baptist Magazine*, November 1868, p. 689.
[41] For an analysis of theological influences, see Roberts, 'The Effect of Charles Finney's Revivalism on the 1858–60 Awakening in Wales', pp. 36–44.
[42] *Evangelical Magazine*, 1860, p. 303.
[43] Kathryn T. Long, *The Revival of 1857–58: Interpreting an American Religious Awakening* (New York: Oxford University Press, 1998), p. 130; Orr, *Fervent Prayer*, pp. 26, 40.
[44] Prime, *Power of Prayer*, pp. 351–2.

7 The Gospel in Society

[1] *Outline of the Lord's Work by the Pastors' College, 1867* (London: Passmore & Alabaster, 1868), p. 69.
[2] *The Sword and the Trowel*, March 1865, p. 130.
[3] *Outline of the Lord's Work by the Pastors' College, 1868*, p. 21; East London Tabernacle (London: East London Tabernacle, 1956).
[4] J. Edwin Orr, *The Second Evangelical Awakening in Britain* (London: Marshall, Morgan & Scott, 1949), p. 97.
[5] Robert Shindler, *From the Usher's Desk to the Tabernacle Pulpit: The Life and Labours of Charles Haddon Surgeon* (London: Passmore & Alabaster, 1892), pp. 142–3.
[6] Orr, *Second Evangelical Awakening*, pp. 97–8.
[7] Richard Cope Morgan, *The Life of Richard Weaver, the Converted Collier* (London: Morgan & Chase, 1861), p. 84.
[8] Orr, *Second Evangelical Awakening*, pp. 99–100.
[9] Hy Pickering, *Twice-Born Men* (London: Pickering & Inglis, 1934), p. 71.
[10] Kathryn T. Long, *The Revival of 1857–58: Interpreting an American Religious Awakening* (New York: Oxford University Press, 1998), pp. 112–13.
[11] Long, *The Revival of 1857–58*, pp. 124–5.
[12] Prime, *Power of Prayer*, pp. 265–7.

13 Long, *The Revival of 1857–58*, pp. 104–5. The letter was printed in the *New York Daily Tribune* of 27 March 1858.

14 Charles Dickens, *All the Year Round*, 5 November 1959, p. 33, cited by Orr, *Second Evangelical Awakening*, p. 177.

15 William Gibson, *The Year of Grace: A History of the Ulster Revival of 1859* (Edinburgh: Andrew Elliott, 1860), pp. 389–91.

16 John Weir, *The Ulster Awakening: Its Origin, Progress, and Fruit* (London: Arthur Hall, Virtue & Co., 1860), p. 192.

17 Weir, *Ulster Awakening*, p. 196.

18 Thomas Phillips, *The Welsh Revival: Its Origin and Development* (Edinburgh: Banner of Truth Trust, 1995, reprint of 1860), p. 103.

19 Phillips, *Welsh Revival*, p. 104.

20 John Kent, *Holding the Fort: Studies in Victorian Revivalism* (London: Epworth Press, 1978), p. 89, citing *The Watchman*, 3 October   1859.

21 John Turnball, 'Eyemouth, Berwickshire', in William Reid (ed.), *Authentic Records of Revival, Now in Progress in the United Kingdom* (London: James Nisbet & Co., 1860), p. 331.

22 Orr, *Second Evangelical Awakening*, p. 214.

23 Weir, *Ulster Awakening*, p. 151.

24 Weir, *Ulster Awakening*, pp. 189–90.

25 Kent, *Holding the Fort*, p. 111.

26 Weir, *Ulster Awakening*, pp. 150–1.

27 Gibson, *Year of Grace*, pp. 163–4.

28 Orr, *Second Evangelical Awakening*, pp. 210–11.

29 Orr, *Fervent Prayer*, pp. 130–1.

30 Annie Trotter, *Lord Radstock: An Interpretation and a Record* (London: Hodder & Stoughton, 1914), p. 15.

31 Trotter, *Lord Radstock*, p. 21.

32 Trotter, *Lord Radstock*, pp. 194–6.

33 Ian M. Randall, *Communities of Conviction: Baptist Beginnings in Europe* (Prague: EBF, 2009), pp. 92–8.

34 Ernest A. Payne, *Freedom in Jamaica* (London: The Carey Press, 1946), p. 88.

35 Orr, *Fervent Prayer*, p. 33.

36 Catherine B. Allen, *The New Lottie Moon Story* (Nashville: Broadman Press, 1980), pp. 34–5.

37 Kenneth Scott Latourette, *A History of the Expansion of Christianity*, Vol. 6 (London: Eyre & Spottiswoode, 1948), p. 336.

38 Robert E. Speer, *George Bowen of Bombay* (New York: printed privately, 1838), pp. 232–3.

39 Paul Harris, 'In Defence of Mass Conversion: John E. Clough and the American Baptist Telugu Mission, 1865–1910', in Ian M.

Randall and Anthony R. Cross (eds), *Baptists and Mission: Papers from the Fourth International Conference on Baptist Studies* (Milton Keynes: Paternoster, 2007), pp. 245–60.

[40] Eugene Stock, *The History of the Church Missionary Society: Its Environment, Its Men and Its Work* (London: Church Missionary Society, 1899), p. 289.

[41] Charles Price and Ian M. Randall, *Transforming Keswick: The Keswick Convention, Past, Present and Future* (Carlisle: Paternoster/OM Publishing, 2000), pp. 105–11.

[42] Orr, *Fervent Prayer*, p. 143.

[43] Brian H. Edwards, *Revival!: A People Saturated with God* (Darlington: Evangelical Press, 1990), pp. 194–5.

8 Conclusion

[1] For example, Ian Stackhouse, 'Revivalism, Faddism and the Gospel', in Andrew Walker and Kristin Aune (eds), *On Revival: A Critical Examination* (Carlisle: Paternoster, 2003), pp. 239–50.

[2] *Christian Advocate*, 28 January 1858, cited by J. Edwin Orr, *The Fervent Prayer: The Worldwide Impact of the Great Awakening of 1858* (Chicago: Moody Press, 1974), p. 42.

[3] J. Edwin Orr, *Fervent Prayer*, p. 197.

[4] *Annual Paper*, 1870, p. 5.

[5] *The Sword and the Trowel*, January 1874, p. 52.

[6] *The Revival*, 19 January 1865, in J. Edwin Orr, *The Second Evangelical Awakening in Britain* (London: Marshall, Morgan & Scott, 1949), p. 77.

[7] Theodore L. Cuyler, *How to be a Pastor* (London: James Nisbet & Co., 1891), pp. 91–2.

[8] Orr, *Fervent Prayer*, p. 200.

Select Bibliography

Anderson, Allan, *Spreading Fire: The Missionary Nature of Early Pentecostalism* (London: SCM, 2007)

Arteaga, William L. de, *Forgotten Power: The Significance of the Lord's Supper in Revival* (Grand Rapids, Mich.: Zondervan, 2002)

Bebbington, David W., *The Dominance of Evangelicalism: The Age of Spurgeon and Moody* (Nottingham: Inter-Varsity Press, 2005)

Bebbington, David W., *Evangelicalism in Modern Britain: A History from the 1730s to the 1980s* (London: Routledge, 1995)

Carwardine, Richard, *Transatlantic Revivalism: Popular Evangelicalism in Britain and America, 1790–1865* (Westport: Greenwood Press, 1978, reprinted by Paternoster, 2006)

Conant, William C., *Narratives of Remarkable Conversions and Revival Incidents* (New York: Derby & Jackson, 1858)

Cooper, Kate and Jeremy Gregory (eds), *Revival and Resurgence in Christian History: Papers Read at the 2006 Summer Meeting and the 2007 Winter Meeting of the Ecclesiastical Society* (Studies in Church History): 44 (Woodbridge: The Boydell Press, 2008)

Davies, R.E., *I Will Pour Out My Spirit: A History and Theology of Revivals and Evangelical Awakenings* (Tunbridge Wells: Monarch, 1992)

Dieter, Melvin E., *The Holiness Revival of the Nineteenth Century* (Metuchen, N.J.: Scarecrow Press, 1980)

Edwards, Brian H., *Revival!: A People Saturated with God* (Darlington: Evangelical Press, 1990)

Evans, Eifion, *When He Is Come: An Account of the 1858–60 Revival in Wales* (London: Evangelical Press, 1967)

Gibbard, Noel, *On the Wings of the Dove: The International Effects of the 1904–05 Revival* (Bridgend: Bryntirion Press, 2002)

Gibson, William, *The Year of Grace: A History of the Ulster Revival of 1859* (Edinburgh: Andrew Elliott, 1860)

Hilborn, David and Ian M. Randall, *One Body in Christ: The History and Significance of the Evangelical Alliance* (Carlisle: Paternoster, 2001)

Holmes, Janice, *Religious Revivals in Britain and Ireland, 1859–1905* (Dublin: Irish Academic Press, 2000)

Hulse, Erroll, *Give Him No Rest: A Call to Prayer for Revival* (Darlington: Evangelical Press, 2006)

Jeffrey, Kenneth S., *When the Lord Walked the Land: The 1858–62 Revival in the North East of Scotland* (Carlisle: Paternoster, 2002)

Kent, John, *Holding the Fort: Studies in Victorian Revivalism* (London, Epworth Press, 1978)

Lloyd-Jones, D. Martyn, *Revival: Can We Make It Happen?* (London: Marshall Pickering, new edition, 1992)

Long, Kathryn T., *The Revival of 1857–58: Interpreting an American Religious Awakening* (New York: Oxford University Press, 1998)

Lovelace, Richard, *Dynamics of Spiritual Life: An Evangelical Theology of Renewal* (Downers Grove, Ill.: InterVarsity Press, 1978)

McLoughlin, William G., *Revivals, Awakenings, and Reform: An essay on religion and social change in America, 1607–1977* (Chicago: University of Chicago Press, 1978)

Murray, Iain H., *Revival and Revivalism: The Making and Marring of American Evangelicalism, 1750–1858* (Edinburgh: Banner of Truth Trust, 1994)

Orr, J. Edwin, *The Fervent Prayer: The Worldwide Impact of the Great Awakening of 1858* (Chicago: Moody Press, 1974)

Orr, J. Edwin, *The Second Evangelical Awakening in Britain* (London: Marshall, Morgan & Scott, 1949)

Phillips, Thomas, *The Welsh Revival: Its Origin and Development* (Edinburgh: Banner of Truth Trust, 1995, reprint of 1860)

Piggin, Stuart, *Firestorm of the Lord: The History of and Prospects for Revival in the Church and the World* (Carlisle: Paternoster, 2000)

Price, Charles and Ian M. Randall, *Transforming Keswick: The Keswick Convention, Past, Present and Future* (Carlisle: Paternoster/OM Publishing, 2000)

Prime, Samuel I., *The Power of Prayer* (New York: Scribner, 1858)

Randall, Ian M., *Spirituality and Social Change: The Contribution of F.B. Meyer (1847–1929)* (Carlisle: Paternoster, 2003)

Randall, Ian M., *What a Friend We Have in Jesus: The Evangelical Tradition* (London: Darton, Longman & Todd, 2005)

Reid, William (ed.), *Authentic Records of Revival, Now in Progress in the United Kingdom* (London: James Nisbet & Co., 1860)

Smith, Timothy L., *Revivalism and Social Reform: American Protestantism on the Eve of the Civil War* (Nashville: Abingdon Press, 1957)

Sprange, Harry, *Kingdom Kids: The Story of Scotland's Children in Revival* (Fearn: Christian Focus, 1994)

Spurgeon, Charles Haddon, *Revival Year Sermons* (Edinburgh: Banner of Truth Trust, 1959)

Walker, Andrew and Kristin Aune (eds), *On Revival: A Critical Examination* (Carlisle: Paternoster, 2003)

Weir, John, *The Ulster Awakening: Its Origin, Progress, and Fruit* (London: Arthur Hall, Virtue & Co., 1860)